The PROMISES of GOD

A
BIBLE
SURVEY

CHRISTOPHER BRYAN CONE TH.D

This book belongs to:
**Adam & Mary
Calvert**

The Promises of God: A Bible Survey
©2005 Christopher Cone
Exegetica Publishing & Biblical Resources
Ft. Worth, TX

2nd Edition 2006

ISBN 0-9765930-0-9

Affectionately dedicated to

My cherished Cathy – Thank you for who you are to me,
and for making this possible. Your love for the Lord brings
me joy. Many have done nobly, but you excel them all.
I love you.

&

My adored Christiana & Cara Grace– I pray that this will
help you both as you seek His face. I hope that it adds to
your joy in studying His Word, and that through it, in some
small way, I may pass along to you an example of His love,
as my blessed parents have tirelessly done for me. I love
you.

TABLE OF CONTENTS

BE DILIGENT TO PRESENT
YOURSELF APPROVED TO
GOD AS A WORKMAN
WHO DOES NOT NEED TO
BE ASHAMED HANDLING
ACCURATELY THE WORD
OF TRUTH.

II TIMOTHY 2:15

INTRODUCTION

The Bible is an amazing Book.
It has been circulated more, read more, and discussed more than any other book in all of history. But it is more than just a book. It is more than just a compilation of stories and narratives and morals and poems.

John Calvin, in his *Institutes of the Christian Religion,* identifies the significance of God's revelation to man in Scripture:

> Therefore, though the effulgence which is presented to every eye, both in the heavens and on the earth, leaves the ingratitude of man without excuse, since God, in order to bring the whole human race under the same condemnation, holds forth to all, without exception, a mirror of His Deity in His works, another and better help must be given to guide us properly to God as a Creator. Not in vain, therefore, has he added the light of His Word in order that He might make Himself known unto salvation, and bestowed the privilege on those whom He was pleased to bring into nearer and more familiar relation to Himself.[1]

What Calvin recognizes is that God's Word is an organized communication of Himself to specific ends. God seeks to be known. After all, John 17:3 tells us that the true meaning of life – even the very definition of life – is to know God. The Bible, therefore, is God's revelation of Himself to mankind, in order that His character may be clearly demonstrated, seen, and to whatever degree He desires, understood.

We are told that 'all Scripture is God-breathed' (II Timothy 3:16). Thus the value of examining the words of Scripture to know Him is great, for they are *His* words – His own accounting of Himself and His plan. His creative work is evident to all, and much of His character and person can be seen in creation itself. As the Psalmist says, 'the heavens are telling of the glory of God'. (Psalm 19:1)

But yet, He has graciously given us so much more than even the artful creation before us. He has graced us with the Word of Truth, that which is useful for teaching, for reproof, for correction, for training in righteousness. For how shall we come to Him if we are not told of Him, and who shall tell us of Him if He does not tell us Himself?

But He does tell us, and just as in creation - we see patterns and organization – we see the same themes of sovereignty and holiness and grandeur running throughout the Bible.

Yet there is one thread running through Scripture that ties it all together. That thread is a key to understanding Scripture as one clear message. It guides us from the opening words of Genesis to the closing 'Amen' of Revelation, and ties them together so beautifully that it is evident that only God could be the Author of such an incredibly divine symphony of life.

God's promises and the fulfillment of those promises form the basic outline of God's communication with man in the Bible. Not only does a Bible survey based on the promises of God give us an outline of Scripture – but also an outline of world history itself - past, present, and future. And more importantly, through the Promises of God, we see the face of The Covenant Keeping God.

Many other signs therefore Jesus also performed in the presence of the disciples which are not written in this book; but these have been written that you may believe that Jesus is the Christ, the Son of God; and that believing you may have life in His name.

John 20:30-31

Meaning of *Bible*: From the Greek singular noun *biblos*, referred to the 11th century use in Egypt of the outer surface of a papyrus reed for writing. Christians later used the plural *biblia* to describe their writings as early as 100AD. This term was transliterated into Old French, and later, modern English.

CHAPTER I
PROMISES PREVIEWED
THE CHRONOLOGY OF THE OLD TESTAMENT

The Old Testament books can be categorized into four different categories: Chronological, Complementary, Wisdom, and Prophetic.

CHRONOLOGICAL BOOKS - There are eleven such books, forming the backbone of the Old Testament, covering 3600 years in chronological order. One leads into the next, and read one after the other, the entire history of the Old Testament would be covered:

Genesis – (4004-1900) – creation, Noah, Abraham, Isaac, Jacob, and Joseph.

Exodus – (1525-1440) – the conclusion of Israel's enslavement in Egypt, the Exodus, and the Mosaic Covenant.

Numbers – (1440-1400) – Israel's 40 years in the wilderness, the two census', one before the wandering, one after.

Joshua – (1400-1370) – Israel's swift, yet incomplete conquest of Canaan.

Judges – (1370-1050) – covers the years that judges ruled Israel.

I Samuel – (1100-1011) – the call of Samuel, the reign of Saul, and the early life of David.

II Samuel – (1011-971) – the reign of David as king over Israel.

I & II Kings – (971-586) – Solomon's kingdom, the divided kingdom, and the beginning of the exile.

Ezra – (538-450) – the spiritual restoration of Israel from the exile.

Nehemiah – (445-433) – the political restoration of Israel from the exile, and chronologically ends the Old Testament.

COMPLEMENTARY BOOKS – They contain accounts of history and cover time periods contemporary to the Chronological Books:

The events of **Job** occur during the time of Genesis.

Leviticus is contemporary to Exodus.

Deuteronomy is the second giving of the Law occurring chronologically in the book of Numbers.

Ruth lived during the times of the judges.

I Chronicles covers the events of II Samuel from a priestly perspective.

II Chronicles deals with the events of I and II Kings from a priestly perspective.

The events of **Esther** took place after the exile.

WISDOM BOOKS – These books were written or compiled primarily during the Monarchy and Divided Kingdom:

Psalms – written primarily by David, some written by Asaph, Moses, and others.

Proverbs – wisdom verses mostly from the pen of Solomon.

Ecclesiastes – an examination of the meaning of life by Solomon.

Song of Solomon – a portrait of marital love, also by Solomon.

PROPHETIC BOOKS – 5 groups of prophetic books written during the Monarchy, Divided Kingdom, and Exile:

A. Prophets to the Nations

> **Obadiah** (840) – message of judgment to Edom.
>
> **Jonah** (780) – a call for repentance to Ninevah.
>
> **Nahum** (650-612) – oracle of judgment against Ninevah.

B. Prophets to the Northern Kingdom of Israel

> **Amos** (755) – judgment, a call to repentance, and promise of future restoration.
>
> **Hosea** (750) – a vivid portrait of God's love toward Israel, despite her unfaithfulness.

C. Prophets to the Southern Kingdom of Judah

    Joel (835) – judgment, deliverance, the Day of the Lord, and future blessing.

    Micah (725) – judgment on the North & South, rebuke of the leaders, and future hope.

    Isaiah (740-680) – the rejection and restoration of Israel by God, and the coming of Messiah.

    Zephaniah (625) – the Day of the Lord: a day of wrath, and a day of restoration.

    Habakkuk (609) – questions of God's sovereignty in dealing with Israel.

    Jeremiah (627-586) – final pronouncements of judgment, promises of future blessing.

D. Prophets during the Exile:

    Lamentations (586) – Jeremiah's mourning over the fall of Jerusalem.

    Ezekiel (593-570) – the sovereignty of God, judgment on Israel, and the future hope of the Kingdom.

    Daniel (536) – God's deliverance of His people, and the timelines.

E. Prophets during the Restoration:

    Haggai (520) – encouragement to complete the temple.

    Zechariah (520-518) – visions, messages, and burdens of hope and redemption for Israel.

    Malachi (450-400) – rebuke of priests, and promise of the forerunner.

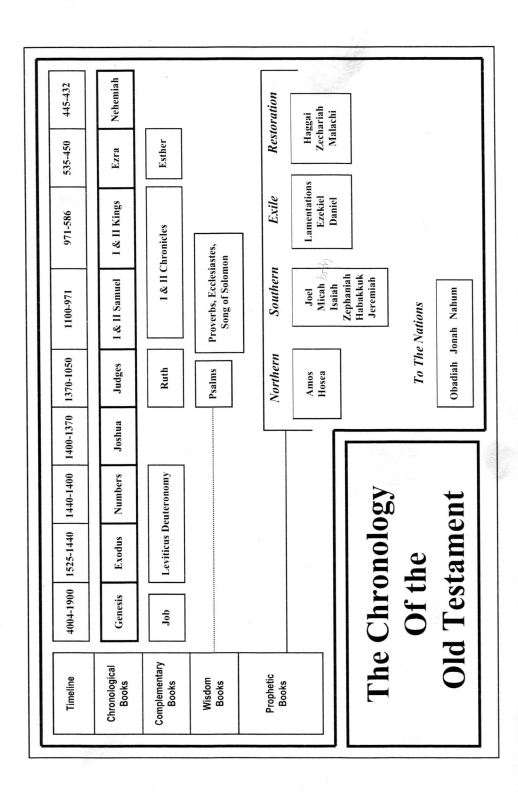

The Hebrew Old Testament

1. The Torah (Law):
Genesis, Exodus, Leviticus, Numbers, Deuteronomy

2. The Nevi'im (Prophets):
A. The Former: Joshua, Judges, Samuel, Kings
B. The Latter: Isaiah, Jeremiah, Ezekiel, The Twelve (Hosea, Joel, Amos, Obadiah, Jonah, Micah, Nahum, Habakkuk, Zephaniah, Haggai, Zechariah, Malachi)

3. The Ketuvim (Writings):
A. Psalms, Proverbs, Job
B. Megillot (Scrolls): Song of Solomon, Ruth, Lamentations, Ecclesiastes, Esther
C. Daniel, Ezra-Nehemiah, Chronicles

*Collectively referred to as the TaNaK, an acronym of the three sections.

Lk24:44

CHAPTER II

PROMISES MADE
CONSCIENCE & THEOCRACY

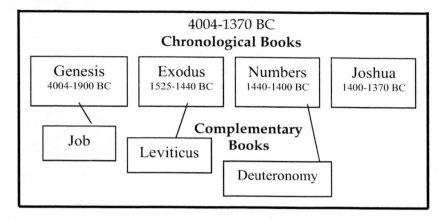

4004-1370 BC
Chronological Books

Genesis	Exodus	Numbers	Joshua
4004-1900 BC	1525-1440 BC	1440-1400 BC	1400-1370 BC

Job

Complementary Books

Leviticus

Deuteronomy

Key Promises

The First Promise: The Need For Redemption ---Gen.2:15-17
The Redemptive Promise: Suffering Messiah --------Gen. 3:15
                                      (3:21; 4:1,25)
The Noahic Covenant ----------------------Gen. 8:21-9:17 (6:5-8)
The Abrahamic Covenant------------Gen. 12:1-3, 15:3-21 (45:5)
The Egyptian Exile & Exodus---------------Gen. 15:13-14 (45:5)
                                      Ex. 6:2-8; 12:12-13,40
The Land Covenant ---------- Gen. 15:18-21; Deut. 30, Josh. 24
Regarding Ishmael ------------Gen. 16:10-14, 21:9-21 (17:17-21)
Regarding Isaac ----------------------------------Gen. 17:17-21
Regarding Jacob & Esau ----------------------------Gen. 25:22-23
To Jacob------------------------------------Gen. 28:10-17 (49:10)
Regarding Judah: Tribe of Royalty --------------------Gen. 49:10
The Mosaic Covenant ----------------------------------Ex. 20-24
The Wilderness Exile -------------------------------Num. 14:28-35
The Exile From The Promised Land ---Lev. 25:1-4; 26:1-46;
Deut. 28-30 (9:4,6) (15:4-5,11)
Failed Conquest -------------------------------------Josh. 23:11-13

Genesis   4004-1800 BC

Creation	The Fall	Abel, Cain & Seth	Noah & The Flood	The Tower Of Babel	To Abraham	To Isaac	To Jacob	To Joseph
1-2	3	4	5-10	11	12-25:11	25:12-27:46	28-36	37-50

1-11 To Man In General

Genesis: God Relates To Man

Key Promises

The First Promise: The Need for Redemption ---Gen. 2:15-17
The Redemptive Promise: A Suffering Messiah ----Gen. 3:15
The Noahic Covenant -------------------------------Gen. 8:21-9:17
The Abrahamic Covenant -------------------Gen. 12:1-3; 15:3-21
The Egyptian Exile & Exodus ----------------------Gen. 15:13-14
The Land Covenant ----------------------------------Gen. 15:18-21
Regarding Ishmael ------------------------Gen. 16:10-14; 21:9-21
Regarding Isaac -------------------------------------Gen. 17:17-21
Regarding Jacob & Esau ----------------------------Gen. 25:22-23
To Jacob --Gen. 28:10-17
Regarding Judah: Tribe of Royalty--------------------Gen. 49:10

Title

The Hebrew title of the book is *bereshith*, the first word in the text, meaning 'in the beginning'. *Genesis* is from the Latin translation of this word, and is also related to the Greek root *genos* referring to lineage and beginnings.

Authorship

Moses' authorship of the Torah (or Pentateuch -the first five books of the Bible) is affirmed throughout Scripture, thus the Biblical literalist will conclude that Moses was indeed the author.

There are numerous claims within the Torah of Mosaic authorship[2], as well as other Old Testament books containing statements of the same[3], and Christ Himself identified Moses as the writer of the first five books on more than 15 recorded occasions[4]. Most significantly, in Luke 24:44, He refers to the entire Old Testament, divided - as the Jews of that day recognized – into three categories: "the Law of Moses and the Prophets, and the Psalms".

Only in recent years has the Mosaic authorship of these books been challenged, most notably by Julius Wellhausen (1844-1918). Wellhausen argued for the Documentary Theory, also known as the JEDP theory – a theory that suggested several men as being responsible for the authorship of the Torah:

"J" is for "Jahwist", as this supposed author seemed to prefer to use the name Jehovah (in Hebrew, Yahweh) in describing God. This author wrote in approximately 850 BC.

"E" is for "Elohist", as this author penned the Hebrew word Elohim when referring to God. His writing was done around 750 BC.

"D" is for "Deuteronomist" – the unnamed redactor of 650 BC, who edited and combined documents "J" and "E" to arrive at the deuteronomic account.

"P" is for the priestly author - primarily of Leviticus – but of other priestly and institutional sections as well.

This form of criticism assumes that because there are variances in the writing 'style' and because there is found within these books a very broad range of subjects, time, and information covered, that it could not possibly be the work of just one author, and the theory dismisses completely the idea of God's inspiring and revealing work.

While Wellhausen was not the primary originator of this theory, he seemed to be it's loudest defender. And the issue at stake is not simply the question of who wrote these books. The process by which Wellhausen and others arrive at their conclusions is a dangerous one, as Gleason Archer points out:

> The Documentary Theory has been characterized by a subtle species of circular reasoning; it tends to posit its conclusion (the Bible is no supernatural revelation) as its underlying premise (there can be no such thing as supernatural revelation)...Unfortunately...it rendered impossible any fair consideration of the evidences presented by the Scripture of supernatural revelation. Furthermore, it made it absolutely obligatory to find rationalistic, humanistic explanations of every miraculous or God-manifesting feature or episode in the text of Scripture.[5]

It is imperative for the Bible student to recognize the conflict between Biblical claims and the claims of liberal criticism. They are mutually exclusive, and as a result, we must make a choice to either acknowledge God's sovereign and supernatural work in revealing Himself, or to thoroughly discount it.

But again, despite any lack of clarity in the arguments or intentions of the critics of Mosaic authorship, the Bible stands clear in its testimony that Moses was the mouthpiece chosen by God to pen the Torah.

Structure

In addition to the topical divisions of Genesis (as shown in the outline chart) the book is also divided into twelve sections, each one (except for the first) beginning with the Hebrew word *toledoth*, 'the generations of'. The *toledoth* divisions are as follows:

1. Creation 1:1 - 2:3 (no *toledoth* introduction)
2. The account of the heavens and the earth 2:4 - 4:26
3. The book of the genealogy of Adam 5:1 - 6:8
4. The genealogy of Noah 6:9 - 9:29
5. The genealogy of the sons of Noah 10:1 -11:9
6. The genealogy of Shem 11:10-26
7. The genealogy of Terah (Abraham) 11:27 - 25:11
8. The genealogy of Ishmael 25:12-18
9. The genealogy of Isaac 25:19 - 35:29
10. The genealogy of Esau 36:1-8
11. The genealogy of the sons of Esau 36:9-43
12. The genealogy of Jacob 37:1 - 50:26

Genesis 1 -11
God Relates to Man in General

The first 11 chapters of Genesis give us the account of God's dealings with mankind in general. Throughout these first chapters, we see God beginning to hone in on specific people through whom He will work His master plan:

Genesis 1-2 record the account of creation, and chapter 2 is highlighted by God's first promise to man:

> And the Lord God commanded the man saying, 'From any tree of the garden you may eat freely but from the tree of the knowledge of good and evil you shall not eat, for in that day that you eat from it you shall surely die.' (2:16-17)

At this early stage in history Adam and Eve had life – they knew God intimately and had a beautiful fellowship with Him. That fellowship was to be maintained and protected simply by obeying one imperative.

Genesis 3 gives us the account of Adam and Eve's failure to keep this command. The consequence was death – immediate spiritual death, and eventual physical death. God had kept His first promise. Mankind was immediately separated from fellowship with God – further demonstrated by God when He banished the first couple from the Garden of Eden. The fellowship was irrevocably destroyed, and man had no ability to correct it.

But even in the tragedy of God's pronounced judgment, He made another promise:

> And I will put enmity between you [the serpent] and the woman, and between your seed and her seed; He shall bruise you on the head, and you shall bruise Him on the heel. (3:15)

As God pronounced judgment on the serpent (Satan, see Rev. 12:9; 20:2), He declared that the seed of woman would execute this very judgment. Note that *seed* here is singular – it references a specific descendant. It later becomes evident that this promise would provide the means to restore the fellowship between God and His created beings.

With each promise made in Scripture, God's plan becomes clearer. In the beginning, the promises seem vague and somewhat mysterious, but as Scripture progresses we find the promises explicitly specific.

Genesis 4 records the tragic murder of Abel by his brother Cain, and again – even as God is judging the wickedness of Cain He makes another promise of deliverance, this one specifically for Cain (4:15).

Genesis 5 gives us the record of the descendants of Adam through Noah – the next man to whom God would make a promise.

Genesis 6 begins with God's lament over what mankind had become:

> Then the Lord saw that the wickedness of man
> was great on the earth, and that every intent of
> the thoughts of his heart was only evil
> continually. (6:5)

The evil on earth had become so great that God would no longer tolerate it. He could perhaps have blotted out mankind entirely and started over – but remember, He had made a promise of deliverance (3:15) that He must keep. God keeps His promises, so God chose a man through whom the thread would continue. That man was Noah.

God's promises do not fail. Even though God would judge mankind by flood, He kept His promise. Genesis 7-8 record the events of the flood and how God remembered the righteousness of Noah, and how He used Noah to save a remnant of the human race, in order to keep His promise.

In Genesis 8 we find that God makes another promise – this one to Noah. The Noahic Covenant is comprised of two parts:

First, is the element of the promise that God made to Himself –

> and the Lord said to Himself, 'I will never again
> curse the ground on account of man, for the intent
> of man's heart is evil from his youth; and I will
> never again destroy every living thing as I have
> done, while the earth remains, seedtime and
> harvest, And cold and heat, and summer and
> winter, and day and night shall not cease.' (8:21b-
> 22)

At this point we now know that God will spare human life and the continuous cycle of life until He has accomplished His purpose – which includes keeping His promises.

Second, is the covenant God makes with Noah:

> ...And I establish My covenant with you; and all
> flesh shall never again be cut off by the water of
> the flood, neither shall there again be a flood to
> destroy the earth. (9:11)

God then refers to this covenant as an "everlasting
covenant between God and every living creature of all flesh
that is on the earth." Once again, God makes Himself
accountable to man by giving His word that He will not
destroy the earth by flood ever again. Imagine the grace of
God – He has all the intrinsic power of being the Creator
and the Almighty, yet He limits what He can and will do –
throughout Scripture – by giving His Word – His promises
to man. This is a theme we will discover often in our study
of the Bible – God willingly limits Himself. By His
declaration that He will do one thing, He eliminates the
possibility that He will do the opposite. And so it is, that the
Almighty God reaches down to us.

It should also be noted, if only in passing at this
point, that the Noahic Covenant also includes some other
significant points: permission to eat meat (9:3-4), and a
mandate for capital punishment as the consequence for
murder (9:6)

Genesis 10 continues on to trace the progeny of Noah.
He had three sons: Shem, Ham, and Japheth.

> These are the families of the sons of Noah,
> according to their genealogies, by their nations;
> and out of these the nations were separated on the
> earth after the flood. (10:32)

Mankind grew numerous, and mighty in unity. Genesis
11 records man's continued defiance of God:
"And they said, 'Come let us build for ourselves a city, and
a tower whose top will reach into heaven, and let us make

for ourselves a name; lest we be scattered abroad over the face of the whole earth.'" (11:4)

This was a direct violation of God's command to be fruitful and multiply, and fill the earth (1:28; 9:1), and it resulted in God taking unique action once again to further His plan. Genesis 11 records the events at the Tower of Babel, where God confused man's languages and destroyed their unity forcing them to scatter and once again submit to the will of the Almighty God.

The chapter closes with the genealogy of Shem, differing from the genealogy in chapter 10 only in that it traces a specific line – the line to Abraham. It is Abraham who would be the instrument God would use to bless all of humanity and keep His promise.

The first 11 chapters of Genesis find God dealing with mankind as a whole. Even the covenant God made with Noah impacted all of creation. Up to this point, God had still not yet made it clear how or through whom He intended to keep His promise of deliverance and redemption. But it is in chapter 12 that the outline of Scripture truly begins to take shape, and out of the shadows will emerge God's grand plan of the ages.

Table of Early Nations

Nation	3000	2500	2000	1500	1000	500	300	0

Sumerians   — 3000-2000 —

Canaanites/ Amorites   — 3000-1450 —

Israelites   ———— 2300-Present ——→

Assyrians   —— 2500-612 ——

Arameans   —— 2500-700 ——

Egyptians   ———— 2300-Present ——→

Ammonites   —— 2500-581 ——

Babylonians   —— 2000-539 —

Philistines   —— 2000-1000 —

Edomites   —— 2000-165 ——

Hittites   — 1900-1180 —

Moabites   1300-600 ——

Phoenecians   1200-332 ——

Persians   800-424 ——

Genesis 12:1-3
The Abrahamic Covenant

If there is a single passage which outlines Scripture, it is Genesis 12:1-3, God's promise to Abraham.

In the previous chapters of Genesis, God has dealt with mankind on a more general basis. Now He chooses one man and directs all of His work with mankind through one promise – the Abrahamic Covenant:

> Now the Lord said to Abram, Go forth from your country, and from your relatives and from your father's house, to the land I will show you; and I will make you a great nation and I will bless you, and make your name great; and so you shall be a blessing; and I will bless those who bless you, and the one who curses you I will curse. And in you all the families of the earth shall be blessed. (12:1-3)

It is important to note that while this covenant was indeed unconditional (once ratified, it was not dependant upon anyone other than God, Who instituted no conditions which could negate the promises He made.), it did hinge initially upon Abraham's obedience to the imperative "Go forth from your country, and from your relatives and from your father's house to the land which I will show you." Abraham was told essentially to leave all that he had known and if he was obedient to this one thing, the covenant would be set in motion. He did, and it was.

The Abrahamic Covenant contains seven specific promises with three general elements.
The *seven promises* are:
1. I will make you a great nation
2. I will bless you
3. [I will] make your name great
4. You shall be a blessing
5. I will bless those who bless you

6. The one who curses you I will curse
7. In you all the families of the earth shall be blessed

The *three general elements* are:
1. people
2. land
3. kingdom

The Promises

I will make you a great nation:
This promise requires that the three elements be in place – a nation cannot be great without people, land, and a kingdom. God's promise entailed innumerable descendants for Abraham, a splendid land (which God would show him), and what would ultimately be an eternal kingdom.

I will bless you:
The promises were not general as God's promises were previously. Rather than being aimed at mankind as a whole, this promise was directed at a specific individual.

[I will] make your name great:
The blessing upon Abraham would be so magnificent that his name would be highly regarded and meaningful in the ages to come.

You shall be a blessing:
Not only would Abraham himself be blessed, but also he would be a blessing to others. In what specific ways and to whom is not defined here, but at the end of 12:3 this blessing shall be expanded and further defined.

I will bless those who bless you:
In addition to the blessings for Abraham and those whom he would be a blessing to, there was a special blessing from God for those who also blessed Abraham. Abraham would hold a special place in the heart of God, and be treated with unique esteem.

The one who curses you I will curse:
In contrast to the blessing for those who bless Abraham is a curse for those who curse him. This will become evident as nations are judged harshly for their treatment of the nation that Abraham fathered.

In you all the families of the earth shall be blessed:
This seventh promise affects not just those who bless or curse, but it will impact people from every nation. Again, no specifics are yet given, but it is evident that not only would Abraham be a blessing (the fourth promise), but through him the entire world would be blessed. It is in this seventh promise that God's earlier promise of redemption (Genesis 3:15) would be kept.

The Elements

People
Genesis 13:16 expands on this element –

> And I will make your descendants as the dust of the earth; so that if anyone can number the dust of the earth, then your descendants can also be numbered.

Land
Genesis 13:14-15 is more specific regarding this element –

> ...Now lift up your eyes and look from the place where you are, northward and southward and eastward and westward; for all the land which you see, I will give it to you and to your descendants forever.

Also Genesis 15:18 –

> ...To your descendants I have given this land, from the river of Egypt as far as the great river, the river Euphrates...

The land element is further expanded in Deuteronomy 30.

Kingdom
Explanation of this element is not found with specificity until it is completely unfurled in the Davidic Covenant of II Samuel 7.

From this point forward, every word of Scripture points forward to the *gradual*, *literal*, and *complete* fulfillment of each of the promises in this covenant.

Genesis 12-25:11
God Relates To Abraham

God initiated His relationship with Abraham by making a covenant with him. Genesis 12-25:11 contain the account of the rest of Abraham's life – an account that further illustrates God's character as the Covenant Keeper.

God tells Abraham to leave his home and follow God to a land that God would show him. Abraham was faithful in this, yet he shows his weakness in other areas. For example, in ch. 12 he does not trust God to protect him from the Egyptians, so he lies. In ch. 16, Abraham does not trust God to provide him with a son as promised. As a result he takes his Egyptian maid as a concubine and she bears him a son, named Ishmael.

God had promised to bless Abraham's descendants, and He indeed would bless Ishmael. Abraham's lack of trust would cause strife for thousands of years between the descendants of Ishmael and those of Isaac.

In spite of Abraham's initial lack of trust, God kept His promise, and in Genesis 21 Isaac is born.

Even at this point, God was not finished teaching Abraham about faith. In Genesis 22 God tells Abraham to sacrifice Isaac as an offering to God.

[note: never in all of Scripture does God request physical human sacrifice, as was the practice of other pagan religions during Abraham's day. God was simply putting Abraham's faith to the test in terms he could understand, as well as providing a divine picture of His plan of salvation for man.]

Abraham was faithful in this. As he was about to commit the act, we are told that the Angel of the Lord (the preincarnate Christ, Himself) stops him, and shows him a ram in the thicket that would take Isaac's place. God provided a magnificent illustration of the work He would do in order to bring fallen mankind back to Himself:
He would give His only Son as a sacrifice.

The ram in the thicket was a substitute for Isaac. Isaac was to die, but by the grace of God there was a substitute. It will soon become clear in the pages of Scripture that Jesus Christ is the Substitute – the Redeemer who would pay for man's sin.

As Abraham's life comes to a close, he was 'satisfied with life' (25:8), as the Lord had blessed him greatly. Even though he was not the perfect example of faith, he was an example nonetheless. Abraham began to understand that God would keep His promises, and even as he saw them begin to unfold in his lifetime (with the birth of Isaac, etc.), there was indeed much more to come.

Through Abraham the promises of God can be traced, and the thread continues with Isaac.

Genesis 15:13-14
The Egyptian Exile and Exodus

As God is ratifying His covenant with Abraham, He adds a bit of strange news:

> Know for certain that your descendants will be strangers in a land that is not theirs, where they will be enslaved and oppressed four hundred years. But I will also judge the nation whom they serve; and afterward they will come out with many possessions. (15:13-14)

Why, after promising to give Abraham's descendants the land would God pull them out again? He says in v. 16 that the "the iniquity of the Amorite is not yet complete". Amazingly, even amidst the wickedness of nations, God shows incredible patience. There was an allotted amount of sin that God would allow the Amorites to commit, and then it would be over. At the right time He would restore the descendants of Abraham to the land, thereby judging the Amorite. We will see this promise fulfilled in Egypt shortly after Joseph's time.

Genesis 15:18-21
The Land Covenant

God adds yet another measure of precision to His covenant with Abraham when He says

> To your descendants I have given this land, from the river of Egypt as far as the great river, the river Euphrates: the Kenite and the Kenizzite and the Kadmonite and the Hittite and the Perizzite and the Rephaim and the Amorite and the Canaanite and the Girgashite and the Jebusite. (15:18-21)

The Land Covenant unquestionably required a literal and physical fulfillment. The boundaries included in this promise are boundaries that Israel to this day has never attained. But God demonstrates patience and a methodical accomplishment of His plan to the extent of completion. His promise will not fail. The descendants of Abraham, through Isaac, will dwell in the land into eternity.

The specific nations mentioned will become significant particularly when the nation of Israel begins her conquest of the land. How will Israel handle these nations? Will it be in accordance with the instruction of the Lord, or will she fall short? This is a key element of the history of Israel, and the question is answered in the latter part of Joshua and the early part of Judges.

Genesis 16:10-14
The Promise Regarding Ishmael

In God's covenant with Abraham, God promised to bless him and make a great nation from him. Abraham tried to force God's hand, becoming the father of Ishmael, a faithless act which would cause many to die throughout the ages. We often recognize Abraham for his faith, but we must also not forget his faithlessness and the consequences it brought .

Because Ishmael was a son of Abraham, God would bless Ishmael. God Himself made that very promise to Hagar, Ishmael's mother:

> I will greatly multiply your descendants so that they shall be too many to count...Behold you are with child, and you shall bear a son; and you shall call his name Ishmael, because the Lord has given heed to your affliction. And he will be a wild donkey of a man, his hand will be against everyone, and everyone's hand will be against him; and he will live to the east of his brothers. (16:10-12)

Ishmael would be the father of a great nation, a nation of violence and strife, as an epic struggle was about to begin.

Genesis 17:17-21
The Promise Regarding Isaac

Ishmael would be blessed by God, but he would not be the son through whom God carried out His Abrahamic Covenant:

> And I will bless her [Sarah], and indeed I will give you a son by her...and you shall call his name Isaac; and I will establish My covenant with him for an everlasting covenant for his descendants after him. And as for Ishmael, I have heard you; behold I will bless him, and will make him fruitful, and will multiply him exceedingly...But My covenant I will establish with Isaac... (17:16b, 19, 20-21a)

Abraham found the promise of a son born to he and Sarah in their old age difficult to fathom, yet God had made the promise, and He intended to keep it. The covenant would be established through Isaac, not Ishmael, but as a result of Abraham's failure, there has been war between the descendants of Isaac and Ishmael, and will be until the Abrahamic Covenant has seen its final fulfillment, as the descendants of Ishmael seek to take what God had promised to Isaac.

Genesis 15:13-14
The Egyptian Exile and Exodus

Abraham's two sons, Isaac and Ishmael would play a vital role in world history. In ch. 25 we find that Ishmael did indeed become the father of a nation and that he brought strife early on – "he settled in defiance of all his relatives" (25:18). God's promise regarding Ishmael was fulfilled, but it was through Isaac that God would fulfill His covenant with Abraham.

Isaac became the father of two sons, Esau and Jacob. They were born a very short time apart from each other, with Esau being the firstborn, and therefore having the rights of inheritance as the firstborn. But God had a different plan, as He told Rebekah:

> Two nations are in your womb; and two peoples shall be separated from your body; and one people shall be stronger than the other; and the older shall serve the younger. (25:23)

Esau placed little value on his inheritance, as he willingly gave it away for some stew (25:25).

Isaac, like his father had a problem with trusting God – he acted in the same manner as Abraham – lying to protect himself in Egypt. This lack of trust notwithstanding, God still kept His promises through these men.

As Isaac neared the end of his days he sought to bless his son Esau, for he loved him, and it was through him that Isaac wished for God to keep His promises. But even in Isaac's desire to bless Esau, the sovereignty of God is evident. God used Jacob's ambitious and deceptive spirit to place a dying father's blessing on Jacob. Isaac, try though he may, could not alter the will of God.

Once again, God had chosen a man to be chosen, and another He chose not to be chosen. God at first chose Isaac, and now He chooses Jacob. As the covenant promises become more specific, so too does the line through whom they would be kept. That the covenant promises would be kept through the line of Jacob becomes even more evident in the next promises God makes.

Genesis 28:10-17
God's Promise to Jacob

> ...I am the Lord, the God of your father
> Abraham and the God of Isaac; the land on
> which you lie, I will give it to you and your
> descendants. Your descendants shall also be
> like the dust of the earth, and you shall spread
> out to the west and to the east and to the north
> and to the south; and in you and in your
> descendants shall all the families of the earth be
> blessed. And behold, I am with you, and will
> keep you wherever you go, and will bring you
> back to this land; for I will not leave you until I
> have done what I have promised you. (28:13-15)

Again, the previous covenants are made more specific. It is
now clear that the covenants run through Jacob. Here God
reiterates the Land Covenant, as well as the seventh
promise of the Abrahamic Covenant – that all families of
the earth shall be blessed through Abraham's descendants,
now, specifically through Jacob's.

Jacob was also granted a unique relationship with God
to this point, even resulting in his name change to Israel
(32:24-28). Israel would become father to twelve sons who
would become the mighty nation named for their father.
And through them, the promises would unfold further still.

Genesis 49:10
Judah: The Tribe of Royalty

The scepter shall not depart from Judah... (49:10)

This is a key promise that directs the future leadership of Israel through the tribe of Judah. Although it will be hundreds of years before this promise will begin to be fulfilled, God once again gives an insight into His plan, and we will see this promise ultimately fulfilled in Christ Jesus.

The Tribes of Israel
Reuben – the firstborn, son of Leah
Simeon – son of Leah
Levi – son of Leah, chosen to be a priestly tribe
Judah – son of Leah, chosen to be the tribe of Messiah, southern tribe
Dan – son of Bilhah (Rachel's maid), northernmost tribe
Naphtali – son of Bilhah
Gad – son of Zilpah (Leah's maid)
Asher – son of Zilpah
Issachar – son of Leah
Zebulun – son of Leah
Joseph – first son of Rachel, favored by Jacob
Benjamin – youngest son of Jacob, by Rachel, southern tribe
Manasseh – firstborn son of Joseph, a half tribe in place of Levi
Ephraim – youngest son of Joseph, blessed by Jacob, half tribe in place of Levi

Job

J o b		1-2	Job's Testing
	Job's Dialogue	3	Job's Lamentation: Better to not have been born
		4-5	Eliphaz Speaks: Unrighteous deserve judgment
		6-7	Job's Response: Proclamation of innocence
		8	Bildad Speaks: God is just, therefore Job sinned
		9-10	Job's 2nd Response: God has not dealt justly
		11	Zophar Speaks: Assertion of Job's guilt
		12-14	Job's 3rd Response: Worthless physicians
		15	Eliphaz' 2nd Speech: Job: Detestable and Corrupt
		16-17	Job's 4th Response: Sorry comforters
		18	Bildad's 2nd Speech: Fate of the wicked
		19	Job's 5th Response: God has wronged me
		20	Zophar's 2nd Speech: Portion of the wicked
		21	Job's 6th Response: God's dealing with the wicked
		22	Eliphaz' 3rd Speech: Yield now to God
		23-24	Job's 7th Response: God's dealing with the wicked
		25	Bildad's 3rd Speech: Man cannot be just
		26-31	Job's 8th Response: I have been righteous
		32-37	Elihu Speaks: God is Righteous
		38-39	God's 1st Rebuke of Job
		40:1-5	Job Responds: Acknowledgment of insignificance
	3-42:9	40:6 – 41:34	God's 2nd Rebuke of Job
		42:1-6	Job Repents
		42:7-9	God Rebukes Eliphaz, Bildad, Zophar
	42:10-17		Job's Restoration

Authorship

Although the author is not identified within the book of Job, likely candidates include Job himself, and even Moses. The timeframe and setting of the book most likely fit into the patriarchal era of Genesis (in part due to the absence of any references to Israelite culture), and the book could have been written between the time of Moses and Ezra, although probably much earlier if authored by Job.

Documentary Or Drama?

Job's existence as a historical person is questioned by some, but Biblical authors refer to him as a historical figure:

> Ezek. xiv. 14 (cf. v. 16-20) speaks of 'Job' in conjunction with 'Noah' and 'Daniel', real persons. St. James (v.11) also refers to Job as an example of 'patience' which he would not have been likely to do had Job been only a fictitious person. Also, the names of persons and places are specified with such a particularity not to be looked for in an allegory.[6]

In addition to the internal evidence for the historicity of Job, there is external linguistic evidence as well – specifically the use of the name 'Iyyob' at such an early date – note that this was also the name of a Syrian prince in the eighteenth century B.C., and also the use of the name Bildad, which was a shortened form of the name Yabil-Dadum, which was found in cuneiform writings during the same period.[7]

The book of Job is more than a divine play or a parable. He is a historical example of God's sovereignty being manifested in the lives of men. The question dealt with is 'Why does God allow the righteous to suffer?' The solution is evident throughout, as man does not have the perspective and cognitive capability to grasp the entirety of God's dealings in any particular situation. He is sovereign. He is omnipotent. He will do as He will, in accordance with His plan.

The book of Job is the perfect prelude to the unfolding of God's promises, as many questions will surely arise in the minds of man in regard to the direction that God has taken or will take in human history. Without a doubt His thoughts are truly beyond human capability, but if we will simply wait upon Him, trusting Him at His word, we will see Him in His glory, and we will grasp at least a fair degree of His purpose in history.

> 'For my thoughts are not your thoughts, neither are your ways my ways', declares the Lord. 'For as the heavens are higher than the earth, so are My ways higher than your ways, and my thoughts than your thoughts.' (Isaiah 55:8-9)

Purpose

God seeks to teach man to have a reliance upon Him despite the *appearance* of circumstances. Job makes two exemplary statements that should be adopted by us all:

> Naked I came from my mother's womb, and naked I shall return there. The Lord gave and the Lord has taken away. Blessed be the name of the Lord. (Job 1:21)

and

> I know that Thou canst do all things, and that no purpose of Thine can be thwarted. Who is this that hides counsel without knowledge? Therefore I have declared that which I did not understand, things too wonderful for me, which I did not know. Hear now and I will

speak; I will ask Thee, and do Thou instruct me. I have heard of Thee by the hearing of the ear; but now my eye sees Thee; Therefore I retract, and I repent in dust and ashes. (Job 42:2-6)

Exodus   1525-1440 BC

Exodus: Israel From Slavery to Freedom	Out of Egypt: Israel Delivered From Slavery 1-15:22	Out of Egypt: Israel Delivered From Slavery	1	Preparation of Israel for Deliverance
			2-4:28	Preparation of Moses
		Moses & Aaron Speak for God 4:29-12:30	4:29-10:29	First Nine Plagues
			11-12:28	Instructions Regarding Passover
			12:28-30	Tenth Plague
		12:31-15:22		Exodus of Israel: Deliverance
	Onward to Sinai: Israel Preserved 15:23-18:27	15:23-27		Rebellion and Provision: Water
		16		Rebellion and Provision: Manna
		17:1-7		Rebellion and Provision: Water
		17:8-16		Battle of Amalek: The Rise of Joshua
		18		Delegation of Authority
	At Sinai: Israel Prepared for the Journey 19-40	19		Preparation for the Law
		Giving Of The Law 20-31	20-24	General Laws
			25-31	Laws Regarding the Tabernacle
		32		Breaking of the Law
		33		Promise of Mercy
		34-35:19		Second Giving of the Law
		35:20-40:33		Obedience to the Law: Tabernacle Built
		40:34-38		The Glory of the Lord Fills the Tabernacle

Key Promises

The Exodus ----------------------------------Ex. 6:2-8; 12:12-13,40
The Mosaic Covenant --Ex. 20

Title

The Hebrew title, *w'ele sh'mot* is the first phrase meaning 'these are the names of'. The English is a transliteration of the Greek word *exodus*, meaning 'a way out'.

Exodus 6:2-8; 12:12-13
The Exodus

In Genesis 15 God had told Abraham that there would be a four hundred year exile for Abraham's descendants. True to His word, the Israelites became slaves in Egypt for a period of 400 years. But God had also said there would be an end to this enslavement, and in Exodus 6:2-8, He pronounces to Moses the nature of this end:

> I am the Lord; and I appeared to Abraham, Isaac, and Jacob, as God Almighty, but by My name, Lord, I did not make Myself known to them. And I also established My covenant with them, to give them the land of Canaan, the land in which they had sojourned. And furthermore I have heard the groaning of the sons of Israel, because the Egyptians are holding them in bondage; and I have remembered My covenant. Say, therefore, to the sons of Israel, 'I am the Lord, and I will bring you out from under the burdens of the Egyptians, and I will deliver you from their bondage. I will also redeem you with an outstretched arm and with great judgments. Then I will take you for My people, and I will be your God; and you shall know that I am the Lord your God, who brought you out from under the burdens of the Egyptians. And I will bring you to the land which I swore to give to Abraham, Isaac, and Jacob, and I will give it to you for a possession; I am the Lord.' (Exodus 6:2-8)

God's deliverance of Israel would include Israel's departure with many possessions (Gen.15), entry into Canaan (Ex. 6:4), and a unique relationship with God (Ex. 6:7).

God's promise of a national deliverance was accompanied by a means for personal deliverance, prefiguring the work of Christ:

> For I will go through the land of Egypt on that night, and will strike down all the first-born in the land of Egypt, both men and beast; and against all the gods of Egypt I will execute judgments – I am the Lord. And the blood shall be a sign for you on the houses where you live; and when I see the blood I will pass over you, and no plague will befall you to destroy you when I strike the land of Egypt. (Exodus 12:12-13)

Here the theme of deliverance requiring blood is echoed. Previously we saw that Cain's sacrifice of the work of his hands was insufficient, whereby Abel's sacrifice – which required the shedding of blood – was acceptable to God (Gen. 4). Then we saw Isaac delivered by the substitutionary death of the ram (Gen. 22). The theme of substitutionary redemption by blood is an important illustration of what Christ would accomplish on the cross, as the substitutionary Lamb who would pay the penalty for sin.

After demonstrating His sovereignty through signs, plagues, and the hardening of Pharaoh's heart, God used Moses to lead Israel out from Egypt, and on toward the Promised Land.

Exodus 20
The Mosaic Covenant

Exodus 20 contains the Ten Commandments, and begins God's covenant with Israel through Moses. The whole of the Mosaic Covenant, spearheaded by the moral laws of Exodus 20, included hundreds of laws (roughly 613) in the categories of moral, civil, and ceremonial.

Perhaps no other covenant in Scripture has been so misunderstood and misapplied. It had a very specific purpose, and it had a very specific scope. It will later be referred to as the Old Covenant, because a New one was necessary to accomplish all that it was not able to. It must also be noted that all that the Old Covenant was unable to accomplish, it was not *intended* to accomplish.

Characteristics of The Mosaic Covenant

National
The covenant was made specifically with Israel, and with no other nation. It was also made with Israel as a whole, not with the individual. National obedience would result in national blessing. For example, consider this well known declaration:

> [if] My people who are called by My name humble themselves and pray and seek My face and turn from their wicked ways, then I will hear from heaven, will forgive their sin, and will heal their land. (II Chronicles 7:14)

This promise of national restoration is followed by a lesser-known promise of national condemnation:

> But if you turn away and forsake My statutes and My commandments which I have set before you and shall go and serve other gods and worship them, then I will uproot you from

My land which I have given you. (II Chronicles
7:19-20a)

Note that punishment and reward deal with Israel's ability
to remain in the land, not with individual salvation or
justification.

Conditional
As evidenced by the subjunctive in Exodus 23:22 'if you will
truly obey his voice and do all I say…" God's covenant with
Israel through Moses was indeed a conditional covenant. It
promised blessing upon the nation if the nation remained
obedient to the law. The converse is thusly true: National
disobedience would be a violation of this covenant, and
therefore, since the covenant was ratified by both parties
involved (God and Israel, Ex. 24:7-8), this same
disobedience would invalidate the contract and make it null
and void. Therefore, God would no longer be obligated by
His word to bless the nation, but would then render
judgment upon the nation, specifically to cast them out
from the Promised Land (Further detail on these conditions
can be found in Leviticus 26). This is the only significant
conditional covenant that God made. The other key
promises rested solely upon Him for their fulfillment.

Physical
The blessings and cursings of the covenant were decidedly
physical. They dealt with God's grace in leading the
Israelites into the land 'flowing with milk and honey'.
Recall II Chronicles 7, which also made it evident that
Israel's ability to dwell in the land was the key issue. It must
then be noted that the Israelites' individual spiritual
conditions were not addressed, nor intended to be
addressed by the Mosaic Covenant.

Unattainable
The Mosaic Covenant never had the ability to bring
redemption, only to point to it and therefore, built into this
covenant was an intended inadequacy that would be

compensated for in other covenants – specifically the New Covenant. God built this covenant to serve its purpose, and once its purpose was complete it was to be replaced, and thereby fulfilled. In hindsight it is evident that God's plan for Israel was to fall short of keeping this covenant. An example of this sovereign intent is found in Deuteronomy 15:4-5, which states,

> However, there shall be no poor among you, since the Lord will surely bless you in the land which the Lord your God is giving you as an inheritance to possess, if only you listen obediently to the voice of the Lord your God, to observe carefully all this commandment which I am commanding you today.

It seems from this passage that Israel had the option of success, but an examination of 15:11, shows otherwise:

> For the poor will never cease to be in the land…

God says again in Deuteronomy 30:11

> For this commandment which I command you today is not too difficult for you, nor is it out of reach…

God made it very clear what He required, understanding the Law would not be difficult. Keeping it would be, however.
Also, note Deuteronomy 30:1:

> So it shall be when all of these things have come upon you, the blessing and the curse which I have set before you, and you call them to mind in the nations where the Lord your God has banished you…

In prophetic voice Moses announces God's promise of restoration, but restoration could not be given unless judgment was first.

God had given the Israelites a Law that they would be unable to keep, and their failure – even though they were held individually and nationally responsible – plays a key role in the fulfillment of God's other promises, the unconditional ones.

The Purpose of The Mosaic Covenant

Reading forward a bit, we find these words:

> Therefore the Law has become our tutor to lead
> us to Christ, that we may be justified by faith.
> (Galatians 3:24)

In short, the Law served to demonstrate that man in all his efforts could not attain to the holiness of God, and therefore, could not receive his deliverance by works. The Mosaic Covenant showed a degree of the true measure of the holiness of God, and man fell far short. Thus, the need for the substitutionary work of Christ becomes clear, and the vague redemptive reference of Genesis 3:15 is unveiled a bit further.

Leviticus

Leviticus: Laws of a Holy God	1-10 Concerning Holy Offerings	For People 1-6:7	1	Burnt Offering
			2	Grain Offering
			3	Peace Offering
			4	Sin Offering
			5-6:7	Guilt Offering
		For Priests 6:8-10:20	6:8-13	Burnt Offering
			6:14-23	Grain Offering / Priestly Offering
			6:24-30	Sin Offering
			7:1-10	Guilt Offering
			7:11-34	Peace Offering
			7:35-38	Explanation
			8-9	Obedience: Aaron as Priest
			10	Disobedience: Nadab and Abihu
	11-22 Concerning Holy People	For People 11-15	11	Regarding Food
			12	Regarding Reproduction
			13-14	Regarding Disease (Leprosy)
			15	Regarding Issue From Men and Women
		16 For Priests:		Regarding the Holy Place
		People & Priests	17:1-9	Regarding Location of Offerings
			17:10-16	Regarding Blood
		For People	18	Regarding Sexual Morality
			19-20	General Laws
		For Priests	21	Regarding Holy People
			22	Regarding Holy Things
		Concerning Holy Times 23-25	23:1-3	Regarding Sabbath
			23:4-8	Regarding Passover
			23:9-14	Regarding Firstfruits
			23:15-22	Regarding Pentecost (50 days)
			23:23-25	Regarding Trumpets
			23:26-32	Regarding Day of Atonement
			23:33-44	Regarding Tabernacles (Booths)
			24	Regarding Lamps, Bread, Punishment
			25	Regarding Jubilee, Sabbatical Year
	26 The Picture of Holiness:			The Mosaic Covenant
	27 The Value of Holiness:			Vows and Tithes

Key Promise

The Exile From The Promised Land-------Lev. 25:1-4; 26:1-46

The Offerings of Mosaic Law						
What	Burnt	Grain	Peace	Sin	Guilt	Ordination
Why	Atonement for the Individual	Reminder of Provision, Gratitude	Remind of Fellowship With God Through Blood	Atonement For Sin of Person, Nation, Priest, or Leader	Atonement For Sin Against Holy Things (Days, Feasts, Tithes,etc.)	Ordination For Aaronic Priesthood
When	Anytime For Sin; Passover, First fruits, Pentecost, Trumpets, Day of Atonement & Booths	Anytime: Gratitude, Commit, Passover, 1st Fruits, Pentecost, Trumpets, Atonement Booths	Anytime For Thanks & To Commit	Anytime For Sin	Anytime For Sin	Consecration of Aaron and His Sons
How	From the Herd, From the Flock, Of Birds	Baked In An Oven, Made On Griddle, In Pan, Of early Ripened Things	Of the Herd, Of the Flock, A Goat	Bull, Goat, Turtle-doves, Pigeons, Flour	A Ram	Various
Where	Leviticus 1,6,23 Numbers 28	Leviticus 2,6,23 Numbers 28	Lev. 3,7	Lev. 4,6,23 Num. 28	Leviticus 5,6,7	Exodus 28 Leviticus 6

Title

The Hebrew title is *w'yiq'ra*, meaning 'and He called', again the first word of the Hebrew text. The English is from the Greek *levitikos*, 'pertaining to the Levites'.

Summary

As a compliment to the book of Exodus, Leviticus provides a dramatic exposition of the Mosaic Covenant. Detailing hundreds of specific laws regarding offerings, moral issues, and calendar emphases, the book further speaks to not only the weighty requirements of the holiness of God, but also contains many types and illustrations of coming fulfillments, always revolving around the central theme of the substitutionary atoning work that Christ would soon (relatively speaking) accomplish.

Leviticus 25:1-4; 26:1-46
The Exile from the Promised Land

A command of great significance is given in Leviticus 25:

> When you come into the land which I shall give you, then the land shall have a sabbath to the Lord. Six years you shall sow your field, and six years you shall prune your vineyard and gather its crop but during the seventh year the land shall have a sabbath rest, a sabbath to the Lord. (Lev.25:2-4)

This law dealt specifically with how Israel was to treat the land she had been given by God. It involved agricultural wisdom, as it would enable the land to be even more prosperous, as well as yet another reminder of the character of God – pointing back to His work of creation, and acknowledging Him as Sovereign over all. This command would be important in deciding how God would judge Israel's failure to abide by the covenant.

The consequences for disobeying the Mosaic Covenant are found in great detail (and harshness) in Leviticus 26, and they included Israel being removed from the land, so that the land could enjoy the sabbath years that Israel would not keep while in the land.

You, however, I will scatter among the nations and will draw out a sword after you, as your land becomes desolate and your cities become waste. Then the land will enjoy its Sabbaths all the days of the desolation, while you are in your enemies' land; then the land will rest and enjoy its Sabbaths. All the days of its desolations it will observe the rest which it did not observe on your Sabbaths, while you were living on it. (Lev. 26:33-35)

and also,

For the land shall be abandoned by them, and shall make up for its Sabbaths while it is made desolate without them. They, meanwhile shall be making amends for their iniquity, because they rejected My ordinances and their soul abhorred My statutes. Yet in spite of this, when they are in the land of their enemies, I will not reject them, nor will I abhor them as to destroy them, breaking My covenant with them; for I am the Lord their God." (Lev. 26:43-44)

This is the promise of a 70 year exile, later identified specifically in Jeremiah 25:11 and Daniel 9:2 which would be "the exact number of years of Sabbaths in 490 years, the period from Saul to the Babylonian Captivity."[8]
Keil and Deilitzsch calculate the numbers exactly:

The term of seventy years mentioned is not a so-called round number, but a chronologically exact prediction of the duration of Chaldean supremacy over Judah. So the number is understood in 2 Chron. 36:21,22; so too by the prophet Daniel, when, Dan. 9:2, in the first year of the Median king Darius, he took note of the seventy years which God, according to the prophecy of Jeremiah, would accomplish for the desolation of Jerusalem. The seventy years may be reckoned chronologically. From the 4th year of Jehoiakim, i.e. 606 B.C., till the 1st year of the sole supremacy of Cyrus over Babylon, i.e., 536 B.C., gives a period of 70 years. This number is arrived at by means of the dates given by profane authors as well as those of the historians of Scripture. Nebuchadnezzar reigned 43 years, his son Evil-Marodach 2 years, Neriglissor 4 years, Labrosoarchad (according to Berosus) 9 months and Naboned 17 years (43+2+4+17 years and 9 months are 66 years and 9 months). Add to this 1 year – that namely which elapsed between the time when Jerusalem was first taken by Nebuchadnezzar, and the death of Nabopolassar and Nebuchadnezzar's accession, - add further the 2 years of the reign of Darius the Mede… and we have 69 ¾ years. With this the Biblical accounts also agree. Of Jehoiakim's reign these give 7 years (from his 4th till his 11th year), for Jehoichin's 3 months, for the captivity of Jehoiachin in Babylon until the accession of Evil-Marodach 37 years (see 2 Kings 25:27, according to which Evil-Marodach, when he became king set Jehoiachin at liberty on the 27th day of the 12th months, in the 37th year after he had been carried away). Thus, till the beginning of Evil-Marodach's reign, we would have 44 years and 3 months to reckon, thence till the fall of Babylonian empire 23 years and 9 months and 2 years of Darius the Mede, i.e., in all 70 years complete.[9]

The precision with which God weaves His historical plan is truly amazing, and it is yet another reason for us to acknowledge His complete sovereignty.

In any case, Israel would break the Mosaic Covenant, and would be subject to the awful consequences. But even amidst the wrath and judgment of God, He would be merciful, and would restore Israel back to the land after 70 years of exile (Lev. 26:44-45).

The Appointed Times of Leviticus 23-25

Name	Time	Description	Purpose
Sabbath	Friday 6:00pm-Saturday 6:00pm	Day of rest on which no work was to be done	1. Rest 2. Illustration of God as Creator
Passover	14th day of the first month (Abib or Nisan), at twilight	Four days of preparation preceded Passover, and it was the precursor to the Feast of Unleavened Bread	1. Illustration of God as Savior 2. Prefiguring of Christ
Feast of Unleavened Bread	15th day of the first month (Abib or Nisan), at twilight	Included a seven day convocation, the 1st and 7th were days of rest, and the days in between featured offerings by fire	Illustration of God as Deliverer (reminder of sudden deliverance of Israel from Egypt)
Firstfruits/ Harvest	The day after the Passover Sabbath	Included burnt & grain offerings established as a perpetual statute	1. Illustration of God as Provider 2. Thanked God in advance for blessing
Pentecost (50 days)	The day after the seventh Sabbath from Firstfruits	Included grain, burnt, & sin offerings, also a perpetual statute	1. Illustration of God as Provider 2. Thanked God for past blessing
Feast Of Trumpets	On the first day of the seventh month	A day of rest and offerings by fire	1. Reminder of God as deliverer 2. Reminder to God of Israel (Numbers 10:10)
Day of Atonement	On the 10th day of the seventh month	A Sabbath of rest, a national humbling of Israel, including offerings by fire	Reminder of God as Atoner, Redeemer, Savior
Feast Of Booths	On the 15th day of the seventh month	An eight day feast during which Israel would live in booths (tents), included an offering by fire, time of rest, and assembly	Reminder of God as Dwelling Place (Ps.90), and God's provision for Israel during and after the Exodus
Sabbatical Year	Every seventh year	A time for the land to rest. No sowing or pruning would take place during this year	1. Reminder of God as Creator 2. Maximized the productivity of the land
Jubilee	Every 50th year	Release of debts, property, and slaves. A year of Redemption	1. God as Judge 2. Brought refreshing, replenishing, and justice

Numbers   1440-1400 BC

Numbers: Bound For The Promised Land	1-10:10	First Numbering: Preparations For The Journey		1-4	The First Numbering
				5-6	Laws of Purity & Sanctity of Israel
				7-8:4	Numberings of Offerings
				8:5-26	Laws of Purity & Sanctity of Levi
				9:1-14	Laws of Passover
			Trumpets 9:15-10:10	9:15-23	The Explanation
				10:1-10	The Instruction
	10:11-14:45	The Journey	1st Journey 10:11-11:34	10:11-36	The Journey
				11:1-34	The Rebellion
			2nd Journey 11:35-12:15	11:35	The Journey
				12:1-15	The Rebellion
			3rd Journey 12:16-14:45	12:16	The Journey
				13:1-25	The Sending of Spies
				13:26-33	The Report of The Spies
				14:1-10	The Response of Israel: Rebellion
				14:11-45	The Judgment of God: Israel Will Wander
	15-19	Preparing For The Wandering		15	Holiness Demanded of Israel
				16:1-40	Rebellion Against Priesthood: Korah, Dathan, Abiram
				16:41-50	Rebellion Against Priesthood
		Authority Of The Priesthood 17-19		17	Attested To: The Rod of Aaron
				18	Explained
				19	Enacted: The Ordinance of the Law
	20-25	The Wandering		20	Sin At Meribah, Harshness of Edom, Death of Aaron
				21	Defeat of Canaan, Rebellion of Israel, Provision,, Sihon & Og
				22-24	Balaam & Barak
				25	Idolatry of Israel, Zealotry of Phinehas
	26-36	Preparations For Entering The Promised Land		26	The Second Numbering
				27	Plea of Zelophehad, Judgment of Moses, Call of Joshua
			Laws 28-30	28-29	Concerning Offerings
				30	Concerning Vows
				31	Defeat of Midian
				32	Settling of Reuben and Gad
				33:1-49	Summary of Journey: Egypt to the Jordan River
				33:50-36:13	Final Instructions

Key Promise

The Wilderness Exile ------------------------Numbers 14:28-35

Summary

The Hebrew title is *b'mid'bar*, which means 'in the wilderness', taken from the first verse, and describing the central theme of the book. The Latin *arithmoi*, translated 'numbers' in English refers to the two numberings of the people taken in the book.

The book of Numbers is named appropriately for the two numberings or censuses of the Israelite people. The first took place as Israel prepared to entered the Promised Land, but due to three rebellions by Israel, God determined that Israel would wander in the wilderness for 40 years, until the rebellious had died. The second census occurred after the 40-year wandering, as Israel once again prepared to enter the Promised Land.

Numbers 14:28-35
The Wilderness Exile

Israel had been prepared by God to enter the Promised Land, yet she rebelled against Him three times, which resulted in the following proclamation:

> Surely all the men who have seen My glory and My signs which I performed in Egypt and in the wilderness yet have put Me to the test these ten times and have not listened to My voice shall by no means see the land which I swore to their fathers, nor shall any of those who spurned Me see it. (Num. 14:22-23)

And again, God expounds on His promise with specificity:

'As I live', says the Lord, 'just as you have spoken in My hearing, so I will surely do to you; your corpses shall fall in this wilderness, even all your numbered men, according to your complete number from twenty years and upward, who have grumbled against Me. Surely you shall not come into the land in which I swore to settle you, except Caleb the son of Jephunneh and Joshua the son of Nun. Your children, however whom you said would become prey – I will bring them in, and they shall know the land which you have rejected. But as for you, your corpses shall fall in the wilderness. And your sons shall be shepherds for forty years in the wilderness, and they shall suffer for your unfaithfulness, until your corpses lie in the wilderness. According to the number of days which you spied out the land, forty days, for every day you shall bear your guilt a year, even forty years, and you shall know My opposition. I, the Lord, have spoken, surely this I will do to all this evil congregation who are gathered together against Me. In this wilderness they shall be destroyed, and there they shall die.' (Num. 14:28-35)

God's character here can be clearly seen. He will not tolerate disobedience, and He will judge it harshly. But even as He judges He shows His mercy, for rather than dismissing the entire nation, thereby breaking His promise, He only judges the current generation, and even in that He is merciful, as he shows mercy to the two men who remained faithful – Caleb and Joshua. Israel would wander for 40 years – the scope of the book of Numbers – and then would return, poised to claim the promise of God.

Deuteronomy

Deuteronomy: 2ⁿᵈ Giving of Mosaic Covenant	**Preface** **1-3**	1	Preparation to Enter The Promised Land
		2:1-15	Wilderness Exile
		2:16-3:29	Conquest Begun & Narrated
	4-11 / **Commandments**	4-5	Call to Obedience: 10 Commandments
		6	Call to Fear God
		7	Call to Purity
		8	Call to Remembrance
		9	Call to Humility
		10	Call to Changed Hearts
		11	Call to Renewal
	Statutes & Judgments **12-27**	12	Regarding Offerings
		13	Regarding Idolatry
		14	Regarding Personal Holiness
		15	Regarding Sabbath Year
		16:1-17	Regarding Passover, Weeks, Booths
		16:18-18:8	Regarding Judges, Justice, Kings & Levites
		18:9-22	Regarding Spiritism & Prophets
		19	Regarding Cities of Refuge, Boundaries, Witnesses
		20	Regarding Warfare
		21	Regarding Crime & Relationships
		22	Regarding Various & Marital Laws
		23	Regarding Countrymen & Foreigners
		24-25	Regarding Marital & Various Laws
		26	Regarding Firstfruits & Tithe
		27	Regarding Curses
	Prologue **28-34**	28-29	Covenant Consequences
		30	Covenant Restoration & Call to Obedience
		31	Commission of Joshua
		32-34	Song, Blessings, & Death of Moses

Key Promises

The Exile From the Promised Land ----------------Deut 28-30
                                    (9:4-6; 15:4-5,11)
The Land Covenant ------------------------------------Deut. 30

Summary

This is the final of the five books of Moses. Titled in Hebrew from *ele ha d'barim*, the first words of the text, meaning 'these the words'. The English is from the Greek *deutero* (second) and *nomos* (law) and refers to the theme of the book, which is the second giving of the Law.

As a complementary book to Numbers, Deuteronomy summarizes briefly the failed initial preparations to enter the land of Canaan and the wilderness exile, and then picks up with Israel's preparations for their second effort to enter the Promised Land. At that point, Moses presents the Law in detail to Israel yet again to remind them of the seriousness of the Covenant which they had entered in to. The reminder of Moses emphasizes the three areas of the Covenant: the commandments (4-11), and the statutes and judgments (12-27). As the reminder was concluded, Moses gave stern warnings regarding failure to abide by the Covenant, as well as profound prophecies regarding Israel's response.

Deuteronomy 28-30 (9:4-6; 15:4-5, 11)
The Exile from the Promised Land

Israel had a tendency to respond with pride to the special stature that they enjoyed, but God reminded them that His choosing of them was based on His sovereignty and not their own national righteousness:

> Do not say in your heart when the Lord your
> God has driven them out before you, 'Because

> of my righteousness the Lord has brought me
> in to possess this land,' but it is because of the
> wickedness of these nations that the Lord is
> dispossessing them before you...Know, then, it
> is not because of your righteousness that the
> Lord your God is giving you this good land to
> possess, for you are a stubborn people. (9:4,6)

God would drive out the nations before Israel, in spite of
Israel's stubbornness. But yet, if Israel remained
disobedient, His patience would end, and they would be
judged. Deuteronomy 15:4, 5, and 11 illustrate the surety of
this. The consequences of disobedience would be intense:

> But it shall come about, if you will not obey the
> Lord your God, to observe all His
> commandments and His statutes with which I
> charge you today, that all these curses shall
> come upon you and overtake you...The Lord
> will make the rain of your land powder and
> dust; from heaven it shall come down on you
> until you are destroyed...So all these curses
> shall come on you and pursue you and
> overtake you until you are destroyed, because
> you would not obey the Lord your God by
> keeping His commandments and His statutes
> which He commanded you. And they shall
> become a sign and a wonder on you and your
> descendants forever. (28:15,24,45-46)

Coupled with Leviticus 25-26, it is evident that the
consequence of disobedience would be a seventy-year exile
from the Promised Land. Yet, even in light of the severity,
the judgment would not completely destroy the nation, as a
remnant would emerge.

> Then you shall be left few in number, whereas
> you were as the stars of heaven for multitude,

because you did not obey the Lord your God. (28:62)

Deuteronomy 30
The Land Covenant (Reiterated)

Genesis 15:18-21 records the land element of the Abrahamic covenant, and Deuteronomy 30 ties this element to future generations of a restored remnant:

> So it shall be when all of these things have come upon you, the blessing and the curse which I have set before you, and you call them to mind in all the nations where the Lord your God has banished you, and you return to the Lord your God and obey Him with all your heart and soul according to all that I commanded today, you and your sons, then the Lord your God will restore you from captivity, and have compassion on you, and will gather you again from all the peoples where the Lord your God has scattered you. If your outcasts are at the ends of the earth, from there the Lord your God will gather you, and from there He will bring you back. And the Lord your God will bring you into the land which your fathers possessed, and you shall possess it; and He will prosper you and multiply you more than your fathers. Moreover the Lord your God will circumcise your heart and the heart of your descendants, to love the Lord your God with all your heart and with all your soul, in order that you may live. And the Lord your God will inflict all these curses on your enemies and on those who hate you, who persecuted you. And you shall again obey the Lord, and observe all

His commandments which I command you today. Then the Lord your God will prosper you abundantly in all the work of your hand, in the offspring of your body, and in the offspring of your cattle and in the produce of your ground, for the Lord will again rejoice over you for good, just as He rejoiced over your fathers; if you obey the Lord your God to keep His commandments and His statutes which are written in this book of the law, if you turn to the Lord your God with all your heart and soul. (30:1-10)

Significantly, God promises both physical and spiritual restoration, reiterating elements of the Land Covenant, that Israel would indeed return to *the* Promised Land.

Key elements of this covenant include:

1. A broken Mosaic Covenant (30:1)
2. Restoration from the worldwide *diaspora*, or scattering (30:3-4)
3. Great blessing in the land (30:5)
4. Spiritual restoration (30:6)
5. Retribution upon Israel's enemies (30:7)
6. Renewed national obedience (30:8)
7. A change of attitude on God's part toward Israel (30:9)

Conclusion

Deuteronomy closes with the song of Moses (32), recounting the mighty and merciful works of God in dealing with Israel; and Moses' blessing of each tribe (33). The account of Moses' death in 34 was possibly written by Joshua.

Joshua   1400-1370 BC

	1	The Leadership of Joshua	
	Central Conquest	2	Rahab: Faith & Reward
		3-4	Crossing Jordan
		5	Circumcision of Israel
		6	Conquest of Jericho
		7	Achan's Sin & Israel's defeat at Ai
	2-10:15	8	Conquest of Ai
		9	Gibeon Deceives Israel
		10:1-15	Israel Defends Gibeon
Joshua: The Incomplete Conquest of Canaan	10:16-43	Southern Conquest	
	11	Northern Conquest	
	12	List of Defeated Kings	
	Land Divided	East of Jordan	13 — Reuben, Gad, Half Tribe of Manasseh
			14 — Caleb
		At Gilgal	15 — Judah
			16 — Half Tribe of Ephraim
			17 — Manasseh (Double Portion)
		At Shiloh	18 — Benjamin
	13-21		19 — Simeon, Zebulun, Issachar, Asher, Naphtali, Dan
			20 — Cities of Refuge (6)
			21 — Cities of the Levites (48)
	Prologue 22-24		22:1-9 Joshuua Addresses Reuben, Gad, Manasseh
			22:10-34 Struggle for Purity: The Misunderstood Altar
			23-24 Joshua's Farewell & Israel's Commitment

Key Promise

Failed Conquest ---------------------------------Joshua 23:11-13

Key Issue

Incomplete Conquest --------------Joshua 15:63; 16:10; 17:13

Authorship

Joshua 24:26 presents Joshua as the primary author, a probability supported by Jewish tradition (i.e., the Talmud). This would place the date of composition right around 1370 BC. The ending (which recorded Joshua's death) could have been written by a later priest or scribe, such as Ezra.

Summary

God's plan to bring Israel into the Promised Land would be continued by His man of choice, Joshua. After a slow start to the conquest, Joshua would lead the nation of Israel on campaigns to the Central, Southern, and Northern parts of Canaan, and the tribes of Israel would receive their inheritance

The nation and her leader were told specifically by God to be thorough in driving out the sinful nations of Canaan:

> When you cross over the Jordan into the land of Canaan, then you shall drive out all the inhabitants of the land from before you, and destroy all their figured stones, and destroy all their molten images and demolish all their high places; and you shall take possession of the land and live in it, for I have given the land to you to possess it. And you shall inherit the land by lot according to your families; to the larger

you shall give more inheritance and to the smaller you shall give less inheritance. Wherever the lot falls to anyone, that shall be his. You shall inherit according to the tribes of your fathers. But if you do not drive out the inhabitants of the land from before you, then it shall come about that those whom you let remain will become as pricks in your eyes and as thorns in your sides, and they shall trouble you in the land in which you shall live. And it shall come about that as I plan to do to them, so I will do to you." (Num. 33:51-56)

Joshua 15:63; 16:10; 17:13
Incomplete Conquest

Israel failed very quickly, as they allowed the Jebusites (15:63), and other Canaanites (16:10; 17:13) to remain – even using some as forced labor. The consequences would be severe.

Joshua 23:11-13
Failed Conquest

So take diligent heed to yourselves to love the Lord your God. For if you ever go back and cling to the rest of these nations, these which remain among you, and intermarry with them, so that you associate with them and they with you, know with certainty that the Lord your God will not continue to drive these nations out from before you; but they shall be a snare and a trap to you, and a whip on your sides and thorns in your eyes, until you perish from off this good land which the Lord your God has given you.

It would not take long for Israel to see the consequences for their failure to drive out the inhabitants of the land. In a matter of a few years, God's promise in this regard would be fulfilled.

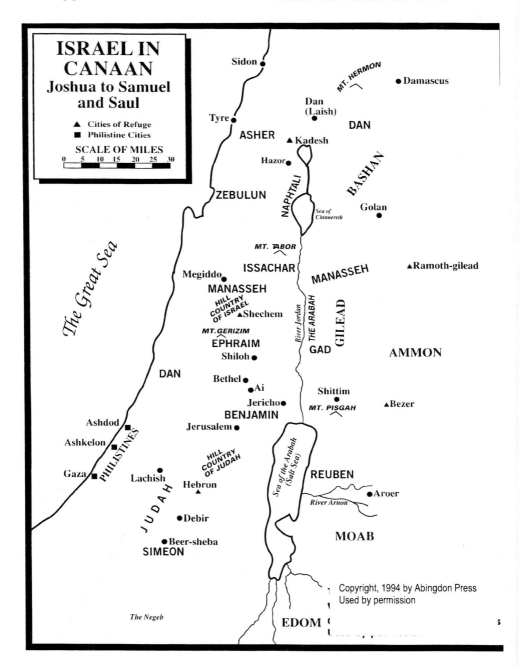

CHAPTER III

PROMISES IGNORED
THEOCRACY REJECTED

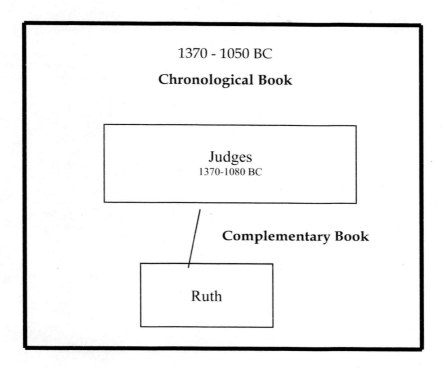

Key Promise

The Mandate For Failed Conquest ----------Judges 1:27-2:23;

(Exodus 23:31-33)

Judges   1370-1050 BC

Judges: Consequences of Incomplete Conquest	Conquest 1:1-3:8	1:1-26	Successful Conquest	
		1:27-3:8	Unsuccessful Conquest	
	The Judges 3:9-16:31	3:9-11	Othniel vs. Mesopotamia (Cushan-rishathaim)	40 years
		3:12-30	Ehud vs. Moab (Eglon) (+18 years before Ehud)	80 years
		3:31	Shamgar vs. Philistines	20 years
		4-5	Deborah & Barak vs. Canaan (Jabin & Sisera)	40 years
		6-8:32	Gideon vs. Midian	40 years
		8:33-9:57	Usurping of Abimalech	3 years
		10:1-2	Tola	23 years
		10:3-5	Jair	22 years
		10:6-12:7	Jephthah vs. Philistines & Ammonites	6 years
		12:8-10	Ibzan	7 years
		12:11-12	Elon	10 years
		12:13-15	Abdon	8 years
		13-16	Samson vs Philistines (+40 years before Samson)	20 years
	Conquest Vs. Impurity 17-21	17-18	Idolatry: Micah & The Tribe of Dan	
		19	The Evil of the Benjamites	
		20	Benjamin Defeated	
		21	Benjamin Preserved	

Key Promise

The Mandate For Failed Conquest -----------Judges 1:27-2:23
(Exodus 23:31-33)

Background

Titled in Hebrew *shophetim,* and Greek *kritai,* both are translated 'judges'. The Talmud attributes the authorship to Samuel, although this conclusion is not a certainty. The book covers a period of 320 plus years.

Summary

Exodus 23:31-33 gives God's mandate that Israel should be thorough in their conquest of the Canaanite nations:

> And I will fix your boundary from the Red Sea to the sea of the Philistines, and from the wilderness to the River Euphrates; for I will deliver the inhabitants of the land into your hand, and you will drive them out before you. You shall make no covenant with them or with their gods. They shall not live in your land, lest they make you sin against Me; if you serve their gods, it will surely be a snare to you.

Unfortunately, Israel failed decisively to obey the command. Judges 1:27-36 lists Israel's failings in this regard. The result was a cycle that continued for over 300 years.

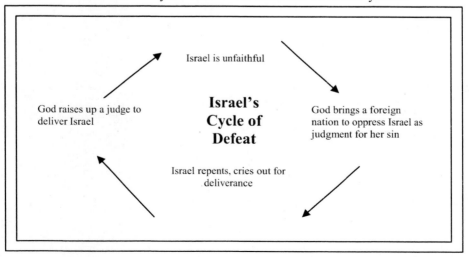

Israel is unfaithful

Israel's Cycle of Defeat

God raises up a judge to deliver Israel

God brings a foreign nation to oppress Israel as judgment for her sin

Israel repents, cries out for deliverance

Israel's failure was twofold: first, they did not completely drive out the nations as they were commanded, and second, just as they were warned, they became involved in idolatry with the nations they allowed to remain, and broke the Mosaic Covenant. As a result, God made it clear that He would not allow further progress for Israel:

> ...'Because this nation has transgressed My covenant which I commanded their fathers, and has not listened to My voice, I also will no longer drive out before them any of the nations which Joshua left when he died, in order to test Israel by them, whether they will keep the way of the Lord to walk in it as their fathers did, or not.' So the Lord allowed those nations to remain, not driving them out quickly; and He did not give them into the hand of Joshua. (Judges 2:21-23)

The cycle of defeat would continue throughout the times of the judges and even into the Monarchy Period.

Ruth

1:1-5 Naomi's Loss	1:6-22 Ruth's Loyalty	2:1-7 Ruth's Diligence	2:8-23 Boaz' Kindness	3 Naomi's Plan: God's Provision	4:1-12 Boaz' Commitment	4:13-17 Obed's Birth	4:18-22 David's Lineage

Ruth: God Protects A Lineage

Key Issues

Lineage of David: Identified and Preserved
Kinsman Redeemer: Portrait of Christ

Background

Named after the primary character, the events of Ruth take place during the time of the Judges – possibly during the time of Gideon, as the events of Ruth occur during a national famine (Ruth 1:1), which was apparently due to Midianite oppression of a sort that was particularly painful for the produce of the land (Judges 6:3-4), prompting God's call of Gideon. Clearly it was not written until the time of David (note that the tracing of David's lineage is a key in the book), with Samuel being a possible author.

Summary

The significance of the narrative can be seen particularly in the advancing and preserving of God's promise regarding the tribe of Judah (Genesis 49:10). God's revelation of promises becomes more specific as time goes on, and the narrative of Ruth builds a bridge in lineage that will ultimately bring about Messiah.

Lineage of David: Identified and Preserved

Both Genealogies of Christ (Matthew's and Luke's) identify Boaz in the line of Messiah, of the tribe of Judah. He was without a wife, and thus childless, at the outset of the narrative. But as the historical account progresses, God uniquely provides a family for Boaz, and the lineage of fulfillment for the Abrahamic promises begins to become evident here, although it is not until II Samuel 7 that we see the true significance.

Ruth is also identified by name in Matthew's genealogy of Christ (Matthew 1:5), which presents to some a quandary in light of the Moabite curse of Deuteronomy 23:3. However, there is no difficulty in consistency here, as it must be noted that the curse referred specifically to the masculine, while Ruth is precisely identified in the feminine (Ruth 1:22). It is also notable that she was daughter in law to Naomi, wife of Elimelech, of the tribe of Judah, and of Bethlehem. Her identification in the Gospel genealogy is significant, as Hebrew genealogies typically did not identify women. Her mention by name is perhaps a Godly reward for her faith in the God of Israel, which resulted in her loyalty and diligence.

Boaz and Ruth are blessed with a child – Obed, who would become the grandfather of David, the next Covenant son of promise.

Kinsman Redeemer: Portrait of Christ

While it is probably not appropriate to see Boaz as a *type* of Christ (since Scripture does not refer to him as such), Boaz demonstrates the Old Testament concept of redemption, serving as a portrait for the later accomplished work of Christ.

Deuteronomy 25:5-10 describes the custom of Levirite marriage, whereby if a brother died childless, his brother would redeem the wife of the dead brother in order to give him an enduring posterity. Boaz carries out this duty for Ruth, and in so doing demonstrates a love and commitment of the same kind as that which is later shown in the redemptive work of Christ.

CHAPTER IV

PROMISES EXPANDED
MONARCHY

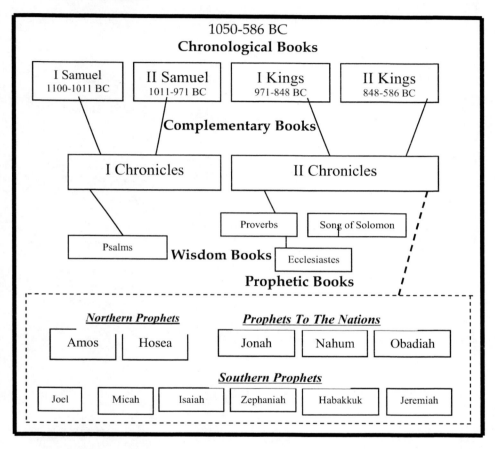

Key Promises

The Davidic Covenant-----------------------II Samuel 7:8-17 (Jeremiah 33, Isaiah 60-66)
To Solomon---I Kings 9:1-9, II Chronicles 7:11-22
The Day of the Lord--Joel 1:15; 2:2, 30-3:3
The Holy Spirit Promised ---Joel 2:28
The Silent Years ---Amos 8:11
The Coming Messiah: Suffering Servant & King ----------------------------------Isaiah 53
The 70-Year Exile --Jeremiah 25:1-14; 29:10-14
Jacob's Trouble --Jeremiah 30:7
The New Covenant --Jeremiah 31:27-40

Rulers of the Monarchy Period & Corresponding Books

			Historical Books	
1040 BC		Saul		
	Wisdom Books	David	**I & II Samuel**	**I Chron**
1000	Psalms, Proverbs			
	Ecclesiastes			
950	Song of Solomon	**Solomon**	I	
	Southern Kingdom: Judah		K	
		Northern Kingdom: Israel	I	
			N	
			G	
	Rehaboam	**Jeraboam**	S	II
	Abijah	**Nadab**		
900	**Asa**	**Baasha**		
		Elahzimel		C
850	**Jehoshaphat**	*Prophets*	**Tibni & Omri**	H
	Jehoram		**Ahab & Ahaziah**	R
	Ahaziah	Obadiah }	**Joram**	O
	Athaliah		**Jehu**	N
800	**Joash**	{ Joel	**Jehoaz**	II	I
	Amaziah		**Jehoash**		C
	Uzziah	Amos }Jonah	**Jeraboam II**		L
		Hosea }	**Zechariah**	K	E
750	**Jotham**		**Shallum & Menahem**	I	S
		{ Micah	**Pekahiah & Pekah**	N	
	Ahaz	{ Isaiah	**Hoshea**	G	
700	**Hezekiah**	{ Zephaniah		S	
	Manasseh	Nahum			
	Amon	{ Habakkuk			
650	**Josiah**				
	Jehoahaz				
600	**Jehoiakim**	{ Jeremiah			
	Jehoiachin				
	Zedekiah				

I Samuel

1100-1011 BC

I Samuel: Transition to Monarchy	1-8:3	The Period of Judges Concludes	1:1-2:10	The Birth of Samuel
			2:11-36	Samuel and Eli's Sons
			3	Call of Samuel
			4-6	The Philistines & the Ark
			7:1-14	God Delivers Israel: Philistine Defeat
			7:15-17	Samuel: Faithful Judge
			8:1-3	Samuel's Sons: Unfaithful Judges
	8:4-31:13	The Monarchy Begins: Saul as King	8:4-22	Israel Seeks a King
			9	Saul Chosen as King
			10	Saul Confirmed as King
			11	Saul Victorious as King
			12	Samuel's Address & Israel's Repentance
			13:1-10	Saul Wars as King (vs. Philistines)
			13:11-23	Saul Acts as Priest
			14:1-46	Saul's Foolishness & Jonathan's Bravery
			14:47-52	Saul's Conquest
			15	Failure & Judgment of Saul
			16	Rejection of Saul: David Anointed
			17	David Confirmed: Defeat of Goliath
			18	David Loved: Jonathan & Michal
			19	David Protected: Saul's Hatred
			20	David Protected: Jonathan's Loyalty
			21	David Provided For: Ahimalech the Priest
			22	Saul's Hatred: Murder of the Priests
			23:1-14	David Victorious: At Keilah
			23:15-29	David Hated: Pursued by Saul
			24	David Merciful: Saul Spared
			25:1	The Death of Samuel
			25:2-44	The Strength of Abigail
			26	David Merciful: Saul Spared
			27	David Afraid: Escapes From Saul
			28	The Wickedness of Saul: Spiritism
			29	David Suspected: By the Philistines
			30	David Victorious (vs. Amalekites)
			31	Deaths of Saul & Jonathan

Authorship

In the Hebrew canon, I & II Samuel were considered to be one book, traditionally recognized as being authored by Samuel (I Samuel 1-24), and Nathan the prophet, and Gad the seer (I Samuel 25-II Samuel), being completed around 975 BC.

Summary

Samuel served as both prophet (3:20) and judge (7:15), bridging the gap from the time of judges to the monarchy period. He presided over a nation who ultimately chose to be 'like the nations' and have a human king (8:5) rather than submit to the loving leadership of God Himself.

Even though God had promised Abraham a nation of descendants, it had not yet been revealed who would rule over this nation. God would use Israel's faulty desire for a human king to ultimately provide the nation with the Divine King. Nevertheless, Israel sought human leadership, continuing their lack of faith (recall Israel's worship of the golden calves while Moses was still on the mountain). They wanted physical signs to verify God's blessing on the nation. This characteristic would be evident in Israel even in the time of Jesus' earthly ministry.

I Samuel records the anointing and coronation of Israel's first human king, Saul of Benjamin. But Saul's inconsistency and ultimate failure to obey God (by assuming the priestly office, and disobedience at Amelek, ch.13 & 15) resulted in God's rejection of this first king. Unlikely David, son of Jessie, of the tribe of Judah was chosen as Saul's replacement. God's choosing of David was further demonstrated by David's victory over Goliath (ch. 17), and God's protection of David from an angry and jealous King Saul.

The book closes with the judgment of Saul for his unfaithfulness, and his death at the hands of the Philistines.

As a prelude to II Samuel, I Samuel narrows the focus to David, chosen by God, who would be the benefactor of another grand promise of God, the Davidic Covenant (II Sam. 7). This covenant would further reveal God's magnificent plan as His Abrahamic promises continued to unfold.

II Samuel   1011-971 BC

II Samuel: David - The Covenant King	Kingdom Divided 1-4:12	1	David Mourns Saul & Jonathan
		2:1-7	David Anointed King of Judah
		2:8-11	Ish-Bosheth King of Israel
		2:12-4:12	Civil War: House of Saul vs. House of David
	Kingdom United 5-14	5:1-5	David Anointed King of Israel
		5:6-25	David's Victories
		6	The Ark Brought to Jerusalem
		7	The Davidic Covenant
		8-10	David's Victories & Kindness to Mephibosheth
		11-12:23	David's Failures: Adultery & Murder
		12:24-25	Birth of Solomon
		12:26-31	David's Victories (vs. Ammon)
		13-14	David's Failure: Family Strife
	Kingdom Endangered 15-20	15-19:7	Absalom's Failed Coup
		19:8-43	David's Reparations
		20	Sheba's Failed Coup
	Kingdom Protected 21-24	21	Gibeonites Receive Justice
		22-23:7	David's Psalm & Last Words
		23:8-39	David's Mighty Men
		24	David's Sinful Census & Repentance

Key Promises

The Davidic Covenant ---------------------------II Samuel 7:8-17

Summary

After the death of Saul, David is made king over the southern tribe of Judah. Saul's surviving son Ish-Bosheth was presented by Abner, the commander of Saul's army as the king of the rest of Israel. After a civil war and the murder of Ish-Bosheth by two of his own commanders, David became king over the entire nation.

In a key conquest of the Jebusites, David captured the city of Jerusalem and made it the new geographical focal point of Israel. He had the Ark of the Covenant brought to Jerusalem and there he planned to build a temple for the Lord.

II Samuel 7:8-17
The Davidic Covenant

In response to David's desire to build the temple, God made a very important promise to David, a promise that would further explain God's intentions and methodology of keeping the Abrahamic Covenant. *The Davidic Covenant contains seven key elements:*

1. "I will make you a great name" (7:9)

Reminiscent of God's promise to Abraham, David is assured of the greatness of his name. Not only would he be renowned in his own generation, but also into eternity.

2. "I will also appoint a place for My people Israel and will plant them that they may live in their own place and not be disturbed again..." (7:10)

This was actually an odd promise in light of Israel's present circumstance. The nation was firmly entrenched in the Promised Land (although they had not yet attained to the borders promised in Genesis 15), and they were beginning a 'golden age'. God's promise to appoint a place and to plant them indicates that they would, at some point between now and then, be taken from the land. Of course that happened with the Exile, but this element includes also the promise that they would not be disturbed again – a national, eternal peace. Israel still awaits this, and as further promises unfold, it will become evident that the Millennial Kingdom of Christ will begin this peace.

3. "I will give you rest from all your enemies" (7:11)

While David did experience some years of peace, his early reign was characterized by war and conquest while his latter reign was filled with family strife – even to the extent of war. The rest and peace David was unable to obtain in his immediate kingdom would be provided on a grander scale.

4. "the Lord will make a house for you" (7:11)

The previous promises required this one. God would provide David an enduring lineage through whom these promises would be kept, and would gain ultimate fulfillment in the Christ.

5. "I will raise up your descendant after you, who will come forth from you, and I will establish his kingdom. " (7:12)

A specific reference to Solomon, God again makes clear that His covenant will be kept through a specific line, and that future establishment of the kingdom of Israel would be through this descendant of David. Some suggest that this element has a near far aspect, that it could be referring both to Solomon, and ultimately to Christ, but this is neither likely (due to the references of committing iniquity in v.14) nor necessary (due to the specific language of the next element in v. 13).

6. "He shall build a house for My name, and I will establish the throne of his kingdom forever" (7:13)

Solomon would build a glorious temple. David here receives consolation, as he wished to build this temple but was forbidden (I Chron. 28), yet he was assured that it would be built and built by his very son.

The second aspect of this promise is very significant. God promises that He would 'establish the throne of his kingdom forever'. Note that it is not the kingdom that is established forever, for then whomever the promise was made regarding would be an eternal king. Rather it is the throne that would be established. There would be One from the line of Solomon, of the line of David, who would rule on this throne into eternity. David understood the significance of this, as he presents his praise to the King who was to come in Psalm 110.

7. "Your throne shall be established forever" (7:16)
Consequently, the throne of David's kingdom would logically be established as well.

Note that none of these promises are conditional. The impetus for their fulfillment was with God and His sovereign working to complete them. They are all precise, and they all would come to pass. Even though David's latter kingdom was marred by revolts, wars, and family strife, He recognized that the Messiah King would come, and in so doing acknowledged that God would keep His promises.

I Chronicles

I Chronicles: The Reign of David	Genealogies & Numberings	1	Genealogy & Descendants of Abraham
		2	Descendants of Jacob
		3	Descendants of David
		4:1-23	Descendants of Judah
		4:24-43	Descendants of Simeon
		5	Descendants of Reuben
		6	Descendants of Levi
		7	Of Issachar, Benjamin, Manasseh, Ephraim, Asher
		8	Descendants of Benjamin
		9:1-34	People of Jerusalem
		9:35-44	Genealogy & Descendants of Saul
	1-10	10	Death of Saul
	The Reign Of David	11-12	David's Kingdom: Anointing, Location, & Support
		13	The Ark Transported: Obed-Edom
		14	David's Kingdom Grows
		15	The Ark Transported: Jerusalem
		16	Celebration of the Ark
		17	Davidic Covenant
		18-20	David's Conquests
	11-21	21	David's Sinful Census
	Preparations For The Temple	22	Solomon Charged to Build the Temple
		23-24	Divisions of Levites
		25	Divisions of Musicians
		26	Divisions of Other Officials
		27	Divisions of Commanders, Officers, & Overseers
		28-29:22	David's Preparations for the Temple
	22-29	29:23-30	Solomon's 2nd Coronation & David's Death

Background

Titled *davari hayami'im* in Hebrew, meaning events or words of the days, the books of I and II Chronicles were united as one in the Hebrew canon as part of the hagiographa – the ketuvi'im. The translator Hieronymus (of the Latin Vulgate) first attributed to the books the title of Chronicles.

Ezra is traditionally regarded as the author, although it is evident that he utilized numerous sources in compiling the book under inspiration of God (see the following:
I Chronicles 29:29; II Chronicles 9:29, 12:15, 16:15, 20:34, 25:26, 33:19).

Due to the priestly authorship (Ezra being both priest and scribe) the Chronicles focus on the primary issues of the reign of David (advancing the covenant promises), the temple preparations, and the spiritual condition of the nation. In contrast to the books of Kings, which focus on the historical exploits of the rulers and the prophets.

I Chronicles parallels the timeframe of the latter parts of I Samuel and the entirety of II Samuel, while II Chronicles parallels the timeframe of I and II Kings. The Chronicles were probably completed approximately 450 BC.

Summary

The first third of the book deals with genealogies and lineages, primarily as introduction to the reign of David, briefly demonstrating how Israel came to that moment.

The Davidic Covenant is recounted in ch. 17, and appropriately the focus then shifts to the preparations for building the temple, including the numbers and divisions of all ministry officers.

The book concludes with David's blessing and prayer regarding the soon to be built temple, and his successor, his covenant son, Solomon.

I Kings   971-853 BC

I Kings: Solomon & The Divided Kingdom	The Kingdom United: The Rule of Solomon	1-11	1	Solomon Becomes King
			2:1-12	David's Charge to Solomon & His Death
			2:13-46	Solomon's Kingdom Established
			3	Solomon Given Wisdom
			4	Solomon's Government
			5-6	Solomon Builds the Temple
			7:1-12	Solomon Builds His House
			7:13-8:66	The Temple Completed & Dedicated
			9:1-9	God's Promise to Solomon
			9:10-10:13	Solomon's Foreign Dealings: Hiram & Queen of Sheba
			10:14-29	Solomon's Greatness
			11	Solomon's Failure & Death
	The Kingdom Divided	12-22	12:1-25	Rehoboam over Judah, Jeraboam over Israel
			12:26-14:20	Jeraboam's Sin, Judgment, & Death
			14:21-31	Rehoboam's Sin & Death
			15:1-8	Abijam King of Judah (evil)
			15:9-24	Asa King of Judah (righteous)
			15:25-31	Nadab King of Israel (evil)
			15:32-16:28	Baasha, Elah, Zimri, Omri: Over Israel (evil)
			16:29-34	Ahab King of Israel (evil)
			17-19	Ministry of Elijah
			20-21	Ahab's Conquests
			22:1-40	Ahab's Defeat & Death
			22:41-50	Jehoshaphat King of Judah (righteous)
			22:51-53	Ahaziah King of Israel (evil)

Key Promises

To Solomon: Established Throne --------------------I Kings 9:1-9

Background

Like Samuel and Chronicles, I and II Kings are one book in the Hebrew canon but were divided later by the Alexandrian translators.

Titled *meleki'im*, meaning kings, the books deal with the monarchy history of Israel, focusing on the kings and prophets, and how Israel journeyed from rich theocracy to enslaved exile.

The authorship of Kings, while not known for certain, has been attributed in Jewish tradition to Jeremiah.

> Jewish tradition credited both 1 and 2 Kings to the prophet Jeremiah (Baba Bathra 15a), and there is much evidence to commend that view. First, Jeremiah lived about the time the book was completed. Second, if Jeremiah were the author, that might explain why the book considers the prophets to be almost as important as the kings. It might also explain how, for example, the author obtained information about Elijah and Elisha. Third, the author's general outlook reminds one of Jeremiah. That is, both this author and Jeremiah understood that idolatry was the main affliction of God's people.[10]

The author utilized several sources (see I Kings 11:41, 14:19, 29) in compiling the book(s), and probably completed the book around 550 BC.

Summary

The first eleven chapters deal with the final period of the United Kingdom, Solomon's reign as king. It was during this period that Israel enjoyed her greatest glory to date. As evidenced by the completing of Solomon's magnificent temple and the time of peace that immediately prefaced and followed.

God reiterated elements of the Davidic Covenant to Solomon (9:1-9), notably that, like David, the throne of Solomon's kingdom would be established forever. However, in 9:5 the statement 'You shall not lack a man on the throne of Israel' lacks the word 'forever' as was present in the previous promise of an eternal throne. For God explained that Israel would be cut off due to idolatry, and the kingdom would be broken temporarily until (as we see later) Israel's Messiah King of the line of David (and Solomon – see Matthew's Genealogy of Christ, Matthew 1:6) would come to restore it.

Just as God had promised, idolatry crept in – even during Solomon's reign, and God began to rip away the Mosaic Covenant blessings of peace and prosperity.

Following Solomon's reign began the Divided Kingdom in 931 BC, which is traced in I Kings from the reigns of Rehoboam in the South and Jeroboam in the North, to Jehoshaphat in the South and Ahaziah in the North. It is notable that during this time the Southern Kingdom of Judah only had two righteous kings, Asa and Jehoshaphat, while the Northern Kingdom of Israel had none – they were all evil.

And despite the ministry of Elijah during this period, Israel's violation of the Mosaic Covenant was nearing its fullness and judgment.

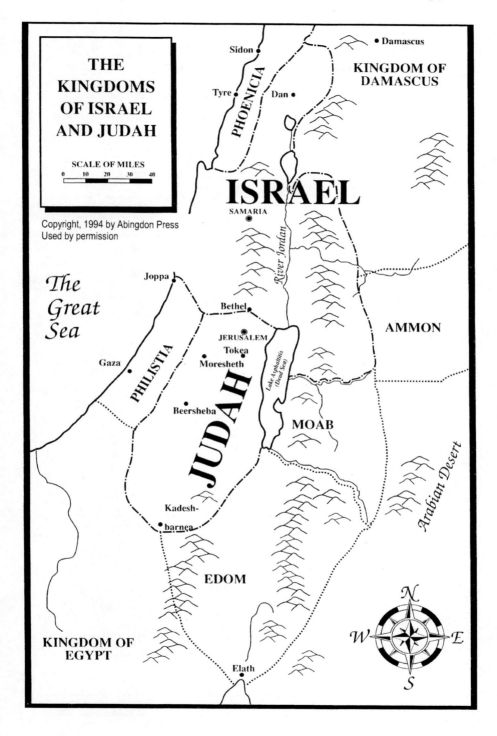

THE
KINGDOMS
OF ISRAEL
AND JUDAH

SCALE OF MILES

0   10   20   30   40

Copyright, 1994 by Abingdon Press
Used by permission

Sidon

Damascus

KINGDOM OF
DAMASCUS

PHOENICIA

Tyre   Dan

ISRAEL

SAMARIA

River Jordan

The
Great
Sea

Joppa

Bethel

JERUSALEM

Tokea

Moresheth

AMMON

Gaza

PHILISTIA

JUDAH

Lake Asphaltitis
(Dead Sea)

Beersheba

MOAB

Kadesh-
barnea

Arabian Desert

EDOM

KINGDOM OF
EGYPT

Elath

N
W   E
S

II Kings   848-586 BC

II Kings: The Monarchy Fails	1-17	The Divided Kingdom	1	Death of Ahaziah
			2	Elisha Succeeds Elijah
			3	Jehoram King of Israel (evil)
			4-8:15	The Ministry of Elisha
			8:16-24	Joram King of Judah (evil)
			8:25-29	Ahaziah King of Judah (evil)
			9-10	Jehu King of Israel
			11:1-20	Athaliah Queen of Judah (evil)
			11:21-12:21	Joash King of Judah (good)
			13:1-9	Jehoahaz King of Israel (evil)
			13:10-13	Jehoash King of Israel (evil)
			13:14-21	Death of Elisha
			13:22-25	God's Compassion: Victories of Jehoash
			14:1-22	Amaziah King of Judah (good)
			14:23-29	Jeroboam King of Israel (evil)
			15:1-7	Azariah King of Judah (righteous)
			15:8-12	Zechariah King of Israel (evil)
			15:13-31	Shallum, Menahim, Pekahiah, & Pekah: of Israel (evil)
			15:32-38	Jotham King of Judah (good)
			16	Ahaz King of Judah (evil)
			17:1-5	Hoshea King of Israel (evil)
			17:6-41	The Northern Kingdom Falls To Assyria
	18-25	The Remaining Kingdom: Judah	18-20	Hezekiah King of Judah (righteous)
			21:1-18	Manasseh King of Judah (evil)
			21:19-26	Amon King of Judah (evil)
			22-23:30	Josiah King of Judah (righteous)
			23:31-35	Jehoahaz King of Judah (evil)
			23:26-24:6	Jehoiakim King of Judah (evil)
			24:7-24:9	Jehoiachin King of Judah (evil)
			24:10-16	Babylonian Exile
			24:17-25:7	Zedekiah King of Judah (evil)
			25:8-21	Babylonian Exile
			25:22-26	Gedaliah Governor of Judah
			25:27-30	Jehoiachin Honored

Summary

Beginning with the death of Ahaziah, II Kings continues the Monarchy narrative. Not only did the early narrative cover transition in the rulership of Israel, there was also significant change in the prophetic leadership of the day, as Elisha succeeded Elijah, whom God took home in the chariot of fire (2:11).

The history of the Divided Kingdom continues with the Northern Kingdom being ruled entirely by evil kings, while the Southern Kingdom did not fare much better. In the case of both the Northern and Southern Kingdoms, their judgment and fall are recorded in II Kings.

The first seventeen chapters conclude with the fall of the Northern Kingdom in 721 BC at the hands of the Assyrians. In addition to the exile the peoples of the North, Shalmanezer (and/or Sargon) brought in Assyrian peoples to inhabit the area of Samaria. The result over the years of the intermarrying between these Assyrians with the Israelites who remained was the cultural disdain during the intertestamental and early New Testament period by the Jews of the progeny, later known as Samaritans. There would be no official return to the land for those of the Northern Kingdom.

The final chapters recount the last kings of Judah and the sieges of Jerusalem by Nebuchadnezzar king of Babylon, who in 605 BC became the dominant world power by defeating Egypt and Assyria (at the Battle of Carchemish).

Nebuchadnezzar's first conquest of Judah came in 605, during the reign of Jehoiakim (24:1-16). Judah became a slave nation until the rebellion of Zedekiah in 597 BC (24:17-25:10), upon which time Nebuchadnezzar came again, this time bringing crippling destruction on the still yet surviving city of Jerusalem – including the burning of the temple and all the great houses of Jerusalem. Finally in 586 BC,

Nebuchadnezzar came a third time, deporting most of the remaining inhabitants.

And so the exile began, just as God had promised. Israel had violated the Mosaic Covenant, and God had passed judgment just as He said He would. But out of the exile would return a remnant that would be the beginning of restoration for the nation.

II Chronicles

II Chronicles: Solomon & The Kings of Judah	The Reign of Solomon	1	Solomon Blessed
		2	Solomon's Preparation For the Temple
		3-5:1	Solomon Builds the Temple
		5:2-14	The Ark & The Glory of God in the Temple
		6-7:10	Solomon Dedicates the Temple
	1-9	7:11-22	God's Promise to Solomon
		8-9	The Greatness of Solomon
	The Divided Kingdom: The Kings of Judah	10-12	Rehoboam
		13	Abijah
		14-16	Asa
		17-20	Jehoshaphat
		21	Jehoram
		22	Ahaziah & Athaliah
		23-24	Joash
		25	Amaziah
		26	Uzziah
		27	Jotham
		28	Ahaz
		29-32	Hezekiah
		33:1-20	Manasseh
		33:21-25	Amon
	10-36	34-35	Josiah
		36:1-9	Joahaz, Eliakim (Jehoiakim), & Jehoiachin
		36:10	Zedekiah, Exile, & Return

Key Promises

To Solomon: Established Throne -----II Chronicles 7:11-22

Background

See I Chronicles.

Summary

Complementing the historical narrative of I and II Kings, II Chronicles concentrates its first nine chapters on the United Kingdom under the reign of Solomon.

Highlighting this section is the account of God's reiteration of the Davidic Covenant to Solomon. Amidst this monologue is found the often-misused conditional terms of judgment and restoration during the Monarchy period under the Mosaic Covenant:

> If I shut up the heavens so that there is no rain, or if I command the locust to devour the land, or if I send pestilence among My people, and My people who are called by My name humble themselves and pray, and seek My face, and turn from their wicked ways, then I will hear from heaven, will forgive their sin, and will heal their land. (7:13-14)

In context these terms of judgment, repentance, and restoration are specifically for Israel under the dispensation of the Mosaic Covenant. Any other application (such as to the church) would be misappropriated.

Chapters ten through the conclusion of the book recount the history of the Divided Kingdom including the fall of kingdoms, the exile, and Cyrus' decree authorizing the first return (36:22-23). It is notable that these last three verses also begin the book of Ezra.

Psalms

Psalms: Communion With God	**1-41** Book 1: David (37), Anonymous (4)	
	42-72 Book 2: David (18), Sons of Korah (8), Anonymous (3), Asaph (1), Solomon (1)	
	73-89 Book 3: Asaph (11), Sons of Korah (4), David (1), Ethan (1)	
	90-106 Book 4: Anonymous (14), David (2), Moses (1)	
	107-150 Book 5: Anonymous (28), David (15), Solomon (1)	

Background

The five-book collection is titled *tihili'im*, meaning in the Hebrew 'praises'. The Greek *psalmoi* provides the origination of the English *psalm*.

The five-part division is from antiquity, and is evidenced by the doxologies that conclude each of the first four sections. Some suggest that this division also mirrors the Torah (also containing five books).

There are numerous authors, as noted above, including: David (73), The Sons of Korah - including Heman, author of Psalm 88 - (12), Asaph (12), Solomon (2), Moses (1), Ethan (1), as well as numerous anonymous or unattributed Psalms (49).

Much of the writing occurred during the Monarchy Period, while the book was probably compiled toward the end of that age, possibly by Ezra[11], or the collection may have been compiled by Solomon, with later additions by the men of Hezekiah.[12] In either case, God has provided an inspirational body of text, preserved through the ages for His glory, and clearly acknowledged to be inspired (Luke 20:42, 24:44; Acts 1:20, 13:33).

Content

Just as the Torah gave God's requirements of a holy and just God, the Psalms give a very vivid portrayal of an intimate God who involves Himself in the emotions and concerns of man. The Psalms present Him as sovereign yet personal, as wrathful, yet merciful. As Psalm 19:7-9 declares,

> The law of the Lord is perfect, restoring the soul; the testimony of the Lord is sure making wise the simple. The precepts of the Lord are right, rejoicing the heart; the commandment of the Lord is pure, enlightening the eyes. The fear of the Lord is clean, enduring forever. The judgments of the Lord are true; they are righteous altogether.

The book of Psalms presents all these elements. In addition to the standard strophe system of Hebrew poetry, the book of Psalms contains the following poetic tools, songs, and instruments, which were used to beautify and embellish the powerful words of praise:

1. psalm – song of praise
2. shiggaion – from the verb, to err, but due to context probably a highly emotional form
3. on the gittith – possibly an instrument or tune that originated from Gath of the Philistines

4. on muth-labben - refers to the youth of a son, and may refer to the treble voice of such

5. on an eight stringed lyre

6. on stringed instruments

7. for flute accompaniment

8. mikhtaim – epigrammatic poem, or atonement Psalm, possibly from the word for gold, *ketem*

9. prayer

10. upon aijeleth hashshahar – possible reference to the help of daybreak, which is illustrative of the theme of the Psalm

11. maskil – contemplative, didactic or skillful Psalm, from the verb ' to make wise'

12. for jeduthun – probably tune or instrument

13. according to the shoshannim – probably tune or instrument

14. set to alamoth - note I Chron. 15:20-21, describing eight Levites playing harps

15. according to mahalath – could reference a tune or instrument

16. according to jonath elem rehoikim – possible reference to a sacrificial dove, or simply a tune or instrument

17. set to al-tashheth – meaning 'do not destroy', and could reference a tune, includes imprecatory Psalms requesting retribution and deliverance from the wicked

18. according to shushan eduth – probably tune or instrument

19. set to el shoshannim eduth – probably tune or instrument

20. according to mahalath leannoth – probably tune or instrument

21. song of ascents – a pilgrimage Psalm, referring to the ascent to Jerusalem

22. selah –pause, crescendo, or a musical interlude

The Messianic Theme

The Messianic idea is a very significant part of the Psalms:

Psalm 2 – deals with the Christ as hated and rejected by the world, as sovereign Judge, King, and Son, and as deserving of the hope of man.

Psalm 8 – refers to the temporary humbling and ultimate exalting of the Christ.
Ascribed to Christ in Hebrews 2:6-8.

Psalm 16:10 – speaks of His resurrection (Acts 13:35).

Psalm 22 – portrayed the anguish of the Christ, as He echoed the opening words on the cross (Matt. 27:46, etc.).

Psalm 31:5 – His last words before dying (Luke 23:46).

Psalm 34:20 – prophetic regarding His bones not being broken (John 19:32-36).

Psalm 38:11-14 - addressed His silence before His accusers (Matt. 26:56, 58-63; 27:11-14, etc.)

Psalm 41:9 – refers to Christ's betrayal by Judas (Matt. 26:20-25).

Psalm 68:18 – refers to His ascension (Ephesians 4:8-10).

Psalm 69 – identifies Christ's zeal for His Father's house in v. 9 (John 2:17), and prophetic of events on the cross in v. 21 (Matt. 27:34, etc.).

Psalm 110 – identifies Christ as King in v. 1 (Matt. 22:44, etc.), and as Priest in v. 4 (Hebrews 5:6, etc.).

From these Psalms referring to the Messiah, much information can be gleaned. Certainly the idea of a suffering Messiah is fully presented, as well as the idea of a sovereign King and an understanding Priest.

This wealth of prophetic information leaves His rejectors without excuse.

Proverbs

Proverbs: The Wisdom of Righteousness			
	Proverbs of Solomon: To His Son 1-9	1-4	Heed Wisdom
		5	Avoid Adultery
		6	Of Diligence, Worth, & Purity
		7	Avoid Immorality
		8-9	Wisdom vs. Foolishness
	Proverbs of Solomon 10-24	10-18	The Righteous vs. The Wicked
		19-24	General Instruction
	Proverbs of Solomon: Transcribed by Hezekiah's Men 25-29	25-26	Moral Comparatives
		27-29	General Instruction
	30		Words of Agur to Ithiel & Ucal
	The Oracle of King Lemuel's Mother 31	31:1-9	The Excellent King
		31:10-31	The Excellent Wife

Background

Titled with the Hebrew *sepher mish'le'i*, the meaning is literally *book of proverbs*.

Several of the authors are named within the book: Solomon, Hezekiah's men, Agur, and King Lemuel; and the book was probably compiled either by Hezekiah's men around 700 BC, or by a later redactor such as Ezra or the like.

Content

The purpose statement of the book appears right away:

> To know wisdom and instruction, to discern the sayings of understanding, to receive instruction in wise behavior, righteousness, justice, and equity; to give prudence to the naïve, to the youth knowledge and discretion, a wise man will hear and increase in learning, and a man of understanding will acquire wise counsel, to understand a proverb and a figure, the words of the wise and their riddles. (1:2-6)

But the theme is found in the following verse:

> the fear of the Lord is the beginning of knowledge; fools despise wisdom and instruction. (1:7)

Therefore, he who would seek after wisdom, must heed the instructions of these proverbs, and consequently will learn of the fear of the Lord. He will gain true wisdom. The Biblical worldview, predicated on the fear of the Lord, is the *accurate* worldview, according to Solomon.

The first nine chapters carry out this idea in Solomon's proverbs to his son (and sometimes sons). He addresses the issue of wisdom, both defining and identifying its true value. In addition, key issues in this section are maintaining purity, diligence, and worth.

A second section begins in ten and continues through twenty-four, and deals initially with a lengthy and thorough contrasting of righteousness vs. wickedness, and concludes with numerous instructions and warnings on sundry topics.

Chapters twenty-five through twenty-nine contain the proverbs of Solomon as transcribed by Hezekiah's men, and deal with moral similes and further moral instruction.

Chapter thirty contains the obscure Agur's oracle to Ithiel and Ucal (perhaps his sons?). The oracle includes a treatise on the character of God, and numerical proverbs of morality.

Finally, the thirty-first chapter is King Lemuel's recounting of his mother's oracle regarding being an excellent king, and identifying an excellent wife.

As the wisest man who ever lived (I Kings 3:12), Solomon rightly identified that a proper perspective of Almighty God is the true essence of wisdom. Without this perspective, the Covenant Promises could not truly be understood, appreciated, or enjoyed, as His character is revealed in each.

Ecclesiastes

1:1-11	Vanity: Nothing New
1:12-18	Vanity: The Earthly Quest For Wisdom
2:1-11	Vanity: Pleasure
2:12-17	Vanity: Wisdom, Madness, Folly
2:18-23	Vanity: Labor
2:24-3:22	Conclusion: The Plan of God
4:1-3	Vanity: Life
4:4-6	Vanity: Works
4:7-12	Vanity: Aloneness
4:13-16	Vanity: Foolishness
5:1-7	Conclusion: Fear God
5:8-20	Conclusion: Enjoy the Gifts of God
6	Vanity: Riches, Wealth, Honor
7-8:5	Conclusion: Advice For Life
8:6-17	Conclusion: The Work of God
9:1-6	Vanity: Life & Death
9:7-10	Conclusion: Enjoy the Gifts of God
9:11-18	Conclusion: Wisdom Better Than Strength
10:1-11	Examples
10:12-14	In Words
10:15-19	In Work
10:20-11:8	Conclusion: Advice For Life
11:9-10	Conclusion: Rejoice
12:1-7	Conclusion: Remember the Creator
12:8-12	Vanity: All Is Vanity
12:13-14	Conclusion: God Is Not Vanity

Ecclesiastes: The Search For Meaning

Background

The Hebrew title is *qoheleth*, for the preacher who identifies himself as the author in 1:1, saying:

> The words of the preacher, the son of David, king in Jerusalem.

The English title Ecclesiastes comes from the Greek word meaning to assemble, referring to the preacher's function which Solomon performed in I Kings 8:1.

While the statement of authorship seems quite self-explanatory, it is not without difficulty:

Due to the presence of Aramaic and even Persian linguistic characteristics within Qoheleth, some suggest a very late date of writing and consequently challenge Solomonic authorship. These criticisms do not seem, however, to consider the possibility that the manuscripts we now possess today could have been copied and even translated to and from Aramaic back into Hebrew during the Exilic or Post-Exilic periods. In any case, the claim for authorship requires the author to have been a king in Jerusalem, which, if not referring directly to Solomon, then it would have been referring to a descendant of David who ruled in Jerusalem, and could have been no later than the 586 BC, a date which would not have allowed for the Persian or Aramaic influences.

It will be suggested here, in agreement with Jewish tradition, that Solomon indeed did author the book during the latter part of his life, no later than around 950-935 BC.

Content

Probably the single most important factor is the repeating of the phrase 'under the sun' which occurs twenty-seven times within the book. The phrase emphasizes an earth-centered perspective, and it bolsters the thesis stated in 1:2, "Vanity of vanities! All is vanity".

Solomon takes his readers on a journey in which he will state, portray, and epitomize personally the truth that without eternal perspective, life is meaningless. He continues in this book what he began, so to speak, in Proverbs, only here, he utilizes more personal narrative.

While his thesis is the hopelessness of life without God, his conclusion is the meaningfulness of every act in life in relation to God:

> The conclusion, when all has been heard, is: fear God and keep His commandments, because this applies to every person. For God will bring every act to judgment, everything which is hidden, whether it is good or evil. (12:13-14)

All too often man seeks to trivialize his life by taking away his responsibility for his actions, by failing to acknowledge his Creator. The search for true fulfillment and happiness cannot be found in this way. Solomon provides living proof that the ways of humanity without God are empty, foolish, and fruitless. The wisest man who ever lived would have us recognize our positionas humble creatures before our Creator. Only then can we truly enjoy the blessings He has prepared for us. Only then can we see Him in all His covenant-keeping glory. To fear God is to possess wisdom and knowledge.

Song of Solomon

Song of Solomon: Be Exhilarated With Her Love	1:1-4a	Bride: Longs For The Groom
	1:4b	Chorus
	1:5-7	Bride: Her Dignity
	1:8-10	Groom: Praise For the Bride
	1:11	Chorus
	1:12-14	Bride: Treasures Her Groom
	1:15	Groom: Praises Her Beauty
	1:16-17	Bride: Praises Him
	2:1	Bride: Fertile & Beautiful
	2:2	Groom: Praises Her
	2:3-6	Bride: Delights In His Affection
	2:7	Groom: Seeks Her Peace
	2:8-13	Bride: The Groom Beckons
	2:14	Groom: Her Form Is Lovely
	2:15	Chorus
	2:16-17	Bride: Admires His Work
	3:1-4	Bride: Seeks & Finds Him
	3:5	Groom: Seeks Her Peace
	3:6-11	Chorus: Solomon's Wedding Day
	4:1-15	Groom: Praises Her Loveliness
	4:16-5:1	Consummation
	5:2-8	Bride: Separation
	5:9	Chorus
	5:10-16	Bride: Praises His Loveliness
	6:1	Chorus
	6:2-3	Bride: Unity & Admiration
	6:4-12	Groom: Praises Her
	6:13	Chorus
	7:1-9	Groom: Captivated By Her Beauty
	7:10-8:3	Bride: Seeks Intimacy With Him
	8:4	Groom Seeks Her Peace
	8:5a	Chorus
	8:5b-7	Love Is Strong
	8:8-9	Chorus
	8:10-14	Bride: Affection & Satisfaction

(Prov. 5:15-19)

Background

Titled in Hebrew *shir hasherim*, the meaning is literally *song of songs*. The title Song of Solomon is due to the claim of authorship found in 1:1, "The Song of Songs which, which is Solomon's"

The book was written by Solomon probably between 975-950 BC.

Content

For some, the subject matter of the Song presents difficulty. If it speaks of a literal relationship, commending marital love, then it is very explicit in nature, and as a result some have shied away from a literal interpretation of the Song as an expression of physical love and affection between a couple.

Two allegorical possibilities have been suggested as alternate understandings: (1) that the Song speaks of God and Israel, or (2) that the Song portrays Christ and the church.

First century Jewish tradition spiritualized the Song, relating it to God's love for Israel, with the verses of the Song tracing Israel's history in relationship to God, while the young church spiritualized it also, but naturally identified it with Christ's love for the church.

Despite the conclusions of these traditions, there is no evidence, internal or external, which would justify an allegorical interpretation. From the text itself, it is clear that Solomon is celebrating the beauty of marital and physical love as a precious gift of God. The lack of simile and allegorical language coupled with the presence of explicit detail regarding physical attribute and affection leaves no doubt as to the Song's meaning.

Recall the words of the same Solomon in Ecclesiastes 4:11,

> If two lie down together they keep warm, but how can one be warm alone?

He again counsels his readers to

> let your heart be pleasant during the days of young manhood. And follow the impulses of your heart and the desires of your eyes. Yet know that God will bring you to judgment for all these things. (Ecc. 11:9).

In like manner he admonishes his son with the following:

> Drink water from your own cistern, and fresh water from your own well. Should your springs be dispersed abroad, streams of water in the streets: Let them be yours alone, and not for strangers with you. Let your fountain be blessed, and rejoice in the wife of your youth. A loving hind and a graceful doe, let her breasts satisfy you at all times; be exhilarated always with her love. (Prov. 5:15-19)

In each of these instances, Solomon describes the importance and beauty of companionship between husband and wife, and the words of the Song only further bolster his message.

Solomon recognizes that in this life God has provided an immeasurable gift – the gift of marital love. He recognizes, perhaps through his own failings and misuses, that the wife of one's youth is to be treasured and enjoyed and that faithfulness to her is the very epitome of honor (Prov. 5,7).

The Song of Solomon is a detailed example of a man and wife cherishing one another through various stages of life. It should serve as a lighthouse of sorts for marriages today.

Although the allegorical conclusions are not appropriate hermeneutically, there can be a secondary tie-in, for as the *Song* helps to strengthen marriages – which serve as picture of of Christ and the church (Eph. 5:31-32) - God's living illustrations (married couples) become an even more beautiful portrayal of His love, further demonstrating His superlative character.

Obadiah   840 BC

Judgment Pronounced	For Pride Against Israel	For Violence to Israel	As Fire	As Possessors	As Judges
1-2	3-9	10-16	17-18	19-20	21

Justice to Edom: Judgment	Mercy to Israel: Exaltation
1-16	17-21

Obadiah: The Justice & Mercy of God

Background

The claim of authorship for the shortest book of the Old Testament is found in 1:1 – "The vision of Obadiah".

This is all that is said about the prophet within the book, and Obadiah is only one of two prophets (Malachi being the other) with no additional biographical information other than their name stated in their prophecies.

Obadiah is a fairly common name in the Old Testament, applying to fourteen people (including this prophet). The author does not seem to be identifiable with any of the other thirteen; therefore we know nothing of identity and background save his name.

The date of the prophecy requires Edomite violence toward Jerusalem, and best fits in context with the events of II Kings 8:20 and II Chronicles 21:16-17, and therefore the date of around 840 BC is ascribed. (Note that Obadiah 11and 13 indicate something far short of a complete destruction of Jerusalem, which might have otherwise indicated a later date of writing, such as 587-586 BC.[14])

Content

Obadiah prophesies judgment against Edom for injustice against Israel. Recall that Edom descended from Esau, and was a source of strife with Israel.

This pronouncement of judgment reminds that God would protect His covenant people Israel, and would keep His promise to Abraham that 'the one who curses you I will curse' (Gen. 12:3).

God's attitude of justice can be clearly seen in v. 15:

> "For the day of the Lord draws near on all nations. As you have done, it will be done to you. Your dealings will return on your own head."

Although directed precisely at Edom, the judgment is a stern warning to all nations who would interfere with the security of God's beloved nation.

Edom's consequences arrived, no later than the time of Malachi (as indicated in Malachi 1:3-5), thus fulfilling yet another promise of God.

Joel   835 BC

1:1-14	1:15-20	2:1-11	2:12-20	2:21-27	2:28-32	3:1-17	3:18-21
Present: On Jerusalem	Judgment Coming	Judgment Described	Judgment Avoidable	Judgment Temporary	Interlude: Times of the Gentiles	Final Judgment	Final Restoration

	Near	Far
1:1-14	1:15-2:27	2:28-3:21

Joel: Judgment & Restoration

Key Promises

The Day of the Lord------------------------Joel 1:15; 2:2, 30-3:3
The Holy Spirit Promised --------------------------------Joel 2:28

Authorship

The author identifies himself as Joel (meaning Yahweh is God), the son of Pethuel. He ministered as a prophet to the Southern Kingdom of Judah, and the book is dated approximately 835 BC. This would make Joel the earliest prophet to the Southern Kingdom. The early date is most probable due to the nations mentioned and the nations excluded from his prophecy (for example, Assyria is not mentioned, although Sennacharib, king of Assyria planned an attack on Judah in the days of Hezekiah, as recorded in II Kings 18-19), and also due to some apparent quotes of Joel by later prophets (Amos 1:2, quoting Joel 3:16; Isaiah 13:6, quoting Joel 1:15).

Summary

These were turbulent times for Israel. The early-mid 9th century BC brought draught and locusts. The political culture of the Southern Kingdom was still intact, but the spiritual culture was steadily failing. It was no coincidence that the land became less and less giving, as the consequences for breaking the Mosaic Covenant were physical.

Joel brings from God an intense message of judgment intermingled with grace, giving elements of present and future, near and far, and indicating key eschatological elements such as the judgments and restoration of Israel, along with the times of the gentiles.

Joel begins with a drastic appeal for the inhabitants of every class in the land of Judah to remember back even to the days of the elders' fathers. He asks "has anything like this happened?" He challenges his audience to think upon the significance of the events taking place, and he details an invasion of locusts – one of epic severity. Four swarms of locusts invaded and were destroying the nations agriculture, a plight which would lead to famine.

It is important to realize that Joel is describing literal events, not painting an allegory. The invasion is presented as literal, and while prophecy can make use of present tense terminology in describing future events, in that type of usage there is always in the context an analogy that connects the terminology to the future. Here there is none. Also, the manner in which these events are described lends evidence to their historicity. Joel makes no use of allegorical language that would imply anything other than a literal event.

Joel then ties the calamity to its cause: he reminds the people that they are God's people. He calls them to wail as a woman betrothed yet without her bridegroom - reminding them of their 'marriage covenant' with God (expounded in Jer. 31:32; Is. 54:5). Joel observes that because rain is being withheld, the vegetation is dried up. Note Joel's emphasis on grain, wine, and oil for offering – these in particular are not available. He says that "the grain offering and the libations are withheld from the house of your God" (1:13b). Encouraged by the wicked leadership of people like Jehoram, Ahaziah, and Athaliah, Judah had been unfaithful to God. She had taken part in all kinds of idolatry, worshipping the false gods of every nation with which she came into contact.

Just as was prophesied in Leviticus 26 and Deuteronomy 11 and 28, God would use the land as a means to judge His faithless people. But God would make another promise -

> If I shut up the heavens so that there is no rain, or if I command the locust to devour the land, or if I send pestilence among My people, and My people who are called by My name humble themselves and pray, then I will hear from heaven and will heal their land. (II Chron. 7:13-14)

God's use of the land to bless and judge Israel was a cornerstone of the Mosaic Covenant, a covenant that Israel had violated. God had called down judgment upon Judah and her land because of her sin, and was now calling the people, through Joel, to humble themselves and pray.

Joel 1:15; 2:2, 30-3:3
The Day of the Lord

The present judgment was merely a precursor to a more significant and severe judgment by God.   In 1:15 Joel introduces one of the most profound events in Biblical prophecy – the Day of the Lord:

> Alas for the day! For the day of the Lord is near and it will come as destruction from the Almighty.

The Day of the Lord encompasses "any period of time however long or short that involves God's direct judgment on the world."[15]

Specifically this is a reference to a definite future time which will begin the tribulation, will include Christ's 2nd Coming, and conclude with His Millennial Kingdom.

> it is concluded that the day of the Lord will include the time of the tribulation. Zechariah 14:1-4 makes it clear that the events of the second coming are included in the program of the day of the Lord. II Peter 3:10 gives authority for including the entire millennium age within this period.[16]

Joel illustrates with clarity that the aspect of the Day to which he refers is a time of future tragedy for Israel, a time that will later be clarified by Jeremiah as "Jacob's Trouble" (Jeremiah 30:7)

With the assurance of coming judgment, Joel paints a horrific picture. He describes the Day of the Lord as a day of darkness and gloom – an event of terror. He describes a great invasion that will be thorough in its destruction of Judah. He seems to be describing an invasion of locusts in terrifying hyperbolic terms, but he does not say that the invaders are locusts as he did in chapter 1. This description emphasizes the invading army being under the authority of God. Note that the invading army of chapter 2 is described with frequent simile that is absent in the description in chapter 1.

> The locust army is regarded as a foretaste of an invading army in the day of the Lord, i.e., in the tribulation period. The future references may be to the demon locusts described in Revelation 9:1-12 and or to the invasion of the king of the North (Ezekiel 38:15, Daniel 11:40)[17]

Joel is describing a day when the judgment of God will be complete, his purpose being to draw Judah into repentance. He calls the nation to return to the Lord with a repentant spirit – "Rend your hearts, not your garments" (2:13). God sought a spiritual humbling. Here would come into play the promise of II Chronicles 7:13-14. Even in a severe time of judgment, God presented an opportunity for grace. If Judah would repent, her land would be restored. And even after the future judgment was to come, God would still restore Judah, and ultimately Israel.

But before that restoration would come remarkable displays of God's greatness and judgment:

> And I will display wonders in the sky and on the earth blood, fire, and columns of smoke. The sun will be turned into darkness, and the moon into blood before the great and awesome day of the Lord comes. (2:30-31)

This passage is quoted by Matthew 24:29, and immediately precedes the coming of the triumphant Messiah King.

The following verse of Joel's exposition is paramount:

> And it will come about that whoever calls on
> the name of the Lord will be delivered. (2:32a)

This is an allusion to the fact that deliverance would be open to the gentiles as well. Paul refers to this passage in his explanation that salvation had indeed come to the gentiles as well (Romans 10:12-13). If this passage was not clear enough on the inclusion of the gentiles in the future, then the preceding promise in 2:28 certainly was.

Joel 2:28
The Holy Spirit Promised

> And it will come about after this that I will pour
> out My Spirit on all mankind;

Peter connects this promise *in kind* to the coming of the Holy Spirit at Pentecost, which signified the birth of the church (Acts 2:16-21). While the scope of this promise extends beyond this singular event (the specific pouring out of 2:28 comes after the initial aspects of the day of the Lord), the prophetic dominoes had begun to fall. The coming of the Spirit and the birth of the church signified the beginning of the last days, which would find their completion in the day of the Lord.

At this day, judgment would be completed and Israel would finally know her full restoration under her triumphant Messiah King.

Jonah   780 BC

Jonah's Call	Jonah's Rebellion	Jonah's Discipline	Jonah's Repentance & Deliverance	Nineveh's Repentance: God's Mercy	Jonah's Anger	God's Rebuke of Jonah
1:1-2	1:3	1:4-17	2	3	4:1-3	4:4-11

Jonah: God's Mercy To The Gentiles: Nineveh

Background

The author is identified in 1:1 as Jonah the son of Amittai, and he ministered during the reign of Jeroboam II of the Northern Kingdom around 780 BC (II Kings14:25).

Content

Jonah was called by God to present a message of repentance and forgiveness to Nineveh, the magnificent capital city of the Assyrian Empire.

Jonah's response to God's willingness to show mercy to gentiles was disobedience, providing an example of the difficulty with which early Jewish Christians would have initially accepting the first gentile converts.

Rather than going east to present God's gracious opportunity to the inhabitants of Nineveh, Jonah fled west to the seaport of Tarshish (in modern day Spain). His disobedience was met with judgment from God, who caused a great storm to oppress the ship he was on, ultimately causing the crew members to recognize Jonah's guilt and to cast him overboard. God's judgment was not without grace, however, as God provided a whale to ingest Jonah thereby protecting him from certain death by drowning. The whale transported Jonah to safety, and after a prayer of repentance, Jonah was released upon dry land.

Again, God called Jonah to go to Nineveh, and this time Jonah submitted, and preached the message of God's judgment upon Nineveh, His desire to show them mercy, and their need for repentance. The people of Nineveh responded humbly with repentance, and God showed them mercy.

Jonah's response was again one of resentment toward God for showing mercy to gentiles. He admitted to fleeing the first time due to fear that God would show them mercy, as he says

> for I knew that Thou art a gracious and compassionate God, slow to anger and abundant in lovingkindness, and one who relents concerning calamity. (4:2)

These words are almost a verbatim quote of Exodus 34:6, making clear the consistent character of God.

In response, God provided Jonah with a unique object lesson. As Jonah watched over the city to see whether or not God would judge it, God provided a plant for Jonah's shelter. Then God brought a worm that destroyed the plant, thus taking away Jonah's comfort and making him angry. God rebuked Jonah with these words:

> Do you have good reason to be angry about the plant?... You had compassion on the plant for which you did not work, and which you did not cause to grow, which came up overnight and perished overnight. And should I not have compassion on Nineveh, the great city in which there are more than 120,000 persons who do not know the difference between their right and left hand, as well as many animals? (4:9-11)

God demonstrated His care even for the gentiles, showing a compassion that would later appear in an even more vivid manner, as the church would demonstrate.

Eventually, the city of Nineveh fell back into its evil ways, including violence against Israel. The prophets Nahum and Zepheniah brought a new message of God's unavoidable judgment to Ninevah (Nahum 1-3, Zephaniah 2:13-15) and just over a hundred years after taking the Northern Kingdom of Israel in conquest (721 BC), the city and the entire Assyrian Empire fell at the hands of Nebuchadnezzar of Babylon along with an alliance of Medes and Scythians in 612 BC.[18]

The Sign of Jonah

Completing Israel's rejection of her Messiah in Matthew 12, the scribes and Pharisees demand from Jesus a sign, and He responds saying:

> An evil and adulterous generation craves for a sign; and yet no sign shall be given to it but the sign of Jonah; for just as Jonah was three days and three nights in the belly of the sea monster, so shall the Son of Man be three days and three

nights in the heart of the earth. The men of Nineveh shall stand up with this generation at the judgment, and shall condemn it because they repented at the preaching of Jonah; and behold something greater then Jonah is here. (Matt. 12:39-41)

Jesus references Jonah and the events of Jonah as a twofold sign condemning Israel's unbelief and unrepentance:

The first element was that Jonah's stay in the belly of the whale portrayed Christ's burial. The second was that even the wicked people of Nineveh repented at the preaching of Jonah, while that generation of Israel reject the preaching of the greatest Teacher of all – their own Messiah.

Amos   755 BC

Amos: Judgment On Nations & Israel	1-2:3 Judgment on Nations	1:1-2	Introduction
		1:3-5	Damascus
		1:6-8	Gaza
		1:9-10	Tyre
		1:11-12	Edom
		1:13-15	Ammon
		2:1-3	Moab
	2:4-9:15 Judgment on Israel	2:4-5	Judah
		2:6-5:3	Israel
		5:4-15	Judgment Still Avoidable
		5:16-20	The Day of the Lord
		5:21-27	God Rejects Israel
		6	God Judges Israel's Arrogance
		7	Amos Intercedes & Amaziah Rejects
		8-9:10	Judgment Unavoidable
		9:11-15	Restoration Assured

Key Promise

The Silent Years --Amos 8:11

Background

The author identifies himself as Amos, a sheepherder from Tekoa (five miles southeast of Bethlehem), who ministered during the reigns of Uzziah king of Judah and Jeroboam II king of Judah. Also he mentions that his prophetic ministry occurred two years prior to the great earthquake mentioned in Zechariah 14:5. Although the exact date of the earthquake is not known, the book is dated around 755 BC, during that latter reign of Jeroboam II.

The calling of Amos is recorded in 7:14-15, as God pulled Amos from his occupation of being a herdsman and grower of sycamore figs, and thrust him into the prophetic ministry with the command to 'Go prophesy to my people Israel.'

Content

Amos' primary ministry was to the Northern Kingdom, although his prophecy begins with numerical oracles of judgment ('for three transgressions and for four...') on various afflicters of Israel, he quickly narrows the focus to the failures of Israel and the coming judgment as consequence.

Amos' prophecy particularly focuses on Israel's violation of the Mosaic Covenant, stating in 2:4 "they have rejected the Torah of Yahweh".

At the outset, this judgment is still avoidable, as the Lord says "Seek Me that you may live". (5:4,6,14) However, the prophetic message of repentance is rejected (7:10-13), and God then makes the judgment assured, as He says "Moreover, Israel will certainly go from its land into exile." (7:17b)

Included in that promise of exile would be a period of silence, a famine for God's word:

> Behold, days are coming", declares the Lord,
> "When I will send a famine on the land, not a
> famine for bread or a thirst for water, but rather
> for hearing the words of the Lord. (8:11).

After the prophetic ministry of Malachi, this promise was kept. God did not speak through any prophet until the coming of John the Baptist as prophesied by Malachi.

Amos' prophecy closes with a message of hope and restoration. God would keep His word. Israel would go into exile. God would be silent for a time. But then, God would be earnest in showing His mercy, and would ultimately restore the fortunes of Israel the restored house of David (9:11).

Hosea   750 BC

1-2:13 Hosea's Commission: A Family of Harlotry: Israel's Unfaithfulness Portrayed	2:14-23 Israel's Restoration	3 God's Faithfulness Portrayed	4-6 Israel's Unfaithfulness	7-13 Israel's Condemnation & Judgment	14 Israel's Restoration

Hosea: God is Faithful Despite Israel's Unfaithfulness

Background

The author identifies himself as Hosea the son of Beeri, and he dates his ministry during the reigns of Uzziah, Jotham, Ahaz, and Hezekiah, kings of Judah, and Jeroboam II, king of Israel. His ministry covers a span of roughly sixty years, and the book is best dated around 750 BC.

Hosea was a resident of the Northern Kingdom (7:5), and his prophetic ministry focuses on that territory. His ministry would prove to be God's last warning to the Northern Kingdom before her destruction in 721 BC, as he was the last prophet who ministered within the Northern Kingdom.

Content

Hosea's focus is on Israel's unfaithfulness in keeping the Mosaic Covenant. God uses him as a living portrayal of that unfaithfulness, commanding him to 'take a wife of harlotry; for the land commits flagrant harlotry' (1:2). Hosea is obedient and takes Gomer the daughter of Diblaim as his wife. The difficulties Hosea encounters in this marriage mirror God's difficulties with unfaithful Israel.

The theme of God as faithful husband to an unfaithful Israel is echoed throughout, and as a result of Israel's unfaithfulness, judgment is pronounced. Yet, even in the midst of judgment, God reiterates there will be a future restoration:

> I will heal their apostasy, I will love them freely. (14:4)

Hosea also acknowledges that one aspect of Israel's restoration would be a return to submission to the house of David, and that in the last days Israel would seek her Messiah King (3:5).

Of Messianic note is 11:1, which says,

> When Israel was a youth I loved him, and out of Egypt I called My son.

At first glance, this seems a casual reference to the nation of Israel and the exodus from Egypt, however Matthew attributes this as referring to the young Christ's flight to Egypt as protection from the evil plot of Herod (Matt. 2:15).

Micah   725 BC

Exile of Israel & Judah	God Will Preserve Israel	Judgment: Leaders, Priests, Prophets	The Last Days: The Just Judge	The Deliverer From Bethlehem	Israel's Unjustifiable Unfaithfulness	Acceptable Offerings To God	Judgment of Israel	The Evil of Israel	Judgment & Restoration of Israel
1	2	3	4 - 5:1	5:2-15	6:1-5	6:6-8	6:9-16	7:1-6	7:7-20

Micah: Israel's Judgment & Hope

Background

The author identifies himself as Micah of Moresheth, a city roughly twenty miles west of Jerusalem, and his prophetic ministry focused on the Southern Kingdom, and covered the reigns of Jotham, Ahaz and Hezekiah, kings of Judah. The judgment upon the North is referred to as still in the future, so the bulk of the book was authored before 721 BC, most likely very near that date, probably 725 BC.

Content

Micah's prophecy addresses primarily Judah, yet includes Samaria as well. It is notable that Micah does not provide a warning *to* the inhabitants of the Northern Kingdom, but rather provides God's pronouncement of judgment *concerning* the territory.

Micah particularly addresses the failed leadership – both spiritual and political – the false prophets, priests, and the heads and rulers. God's judgment would be particularly stern with them.

God's plan of restoration is also clearly communicated, as the last days judgment and restoration of Israel is described in ch. 4.

As always, God's plan of restoration centers on the Messianic hope, which is again mentioned in 5:2-5a:

> But as for you, Bethlehem Ephrathah, too little to be among the clans of Judah, from you One will go forth for Me to be ruler in Israel. His goings forth are from long ago, from the days of eternity…and He will arise and shepherd His flock…and this One will be our peace.

Matthew identifies that the chief priests and scribes recognized that this spoke of Messiah (Matt. 2:5-6).

Even before the exile judgment on Israel, God had already provided the Israelites with the hope of restoration and the knowledge of a coming Messiah, both to suffer and redeem, and to restore the nation as King.

Isaiah   740-680 BC

Isaiah: The Salvation of God – The Holy One of Israel	1-39 Rejection By God	1-6 Condemnation, Consummation, & Commission
		7-12 Coming of Messiah
		13-23 Condemnation of Nations: Oracles/Burdens
		24-27 Coming Tribulation & Triumph
		28-33 Condemnation (Woes) & Consummation
		34-35 Condemnation & Consummation
		36-39 Chronicle of Mercy
	40-66 Restoration By God	40-48 A Sovereign Redeemer
		49-57 A Servant Redeemer
		58-66 A Ruling Redeemer

Key Promise

The Messiah: Suffering Servant and King ------------Isaiah 53

Background

Isaiah identifies himself as the son of Amoz, and the scope of his ministry as during the reigns of Uzziah, Jotham, Ahaz, and Hezekiah, kings of Judah, the territory to whom Isaiah ministered (1:1). His ministry spanned roughly sixty years, from about 740-680.

Jewish tradition held that he was a member of a royal family, and that he was killed during the reign of Manasseh very violently, as a result of his godly ministry.[19]

Because of the predictive nature of Isaiah's ministry, some modern (as early as the late eighteenth century) critics have promoted a documentary theory regarding the authorship of Isaiah. It is suggested that in addition to the historical Isaiah, who authored the first thirty-nine chapters, there was a redactor who lived in Babylon after the fall of Jerusalem who completed the latter part of the book (thereby justifying prophetic mentions of the coming fall of the city), and who is commonly referred to as Deutero-Isaiah. Some even refer to a third author, Trito-Isaiah. These critical methods are unjustifiable and simply seek to explain away the miraculous aspect of predictive prophecy with which God revealed His plan.

However, Jewish tradition as well as New Testament writers acknowledge the genuineness of Isaiah's authorship:

Matthew attributes Isaiah 40:3 and 42:1 to Isaiah (Matt. 3:3, and 12:17-18). Luke recognizes Isaiah's authorship of 40:3-5 (Luke 3:4) and 53:7-8 (Acts 8:28). Paul also acknowledges that Isaiah wrote the latter portion of the book, attributing Isaiah 53:1 and 65:1 to Isaiah (Romans 10:16,20).

The authority and legitimacy of Isaiah's authorship was further verified by Christ Himself, as He quoted both the earlier section of the book (Isaiah 29:13 in Matthew 15:8-9), and the latter part of the book (Isaiah 61:1 in Matthew 11:5), as authentic and prophetic of Himself.

Content

Isaiah's call is found in ch. 6, which also contains a key descriptive of the character of God.

In both the Hebrew and Greek languages, repetition is a significant point of emphasis, and Isaiah 6:3 contains the only description of God that is repeated three times in immediate succession:

"Holy, holy, holy, is the Lord of Hosts." The angels who are certainly acquainted with His character echo the words here. The description is also found in Revelation 4:8, spoken by the four living creatures before His throne.

To understand God and His plan, He must be seen as holy above all. His attributes of love and mercy, of wrath and justice, all flow from His holiness. This is the characteristic that explains the Covenants and demonstrates the purpose of His plan.

Chapters 1-35 provide a thorough message of judgment upon Israel and the nations, interspersed with an equally merciful message of restoration.

Chapters 36-39 contain a historical interlude, recounting the invasion and miraculous defeat of the Assyrians led by Sennacherib, in 690 BC, as well as the merciful healing of Hezekiah. This narrative is a parallel to II Kings 18-20 and II Chronicles 32.

Chapters 40-66 further advance the prophecies of Israel's restoration.

The Messianic Message

While Isaiah's prophecy contains the message of judgment and ultimate restoration, his is primarily a Messianic prophecy, some of which includes:

1:18 -Salvation by Messiah is alluded to.

7:14-16 -Messiah's virgin birth is prophesied.

9:1-7 – The Light of the World & The Prince of Peace.

11 – The Shoot of Jessie & His coming Kingdom.

40 – His forerunner, the Word, the Shepherd, the Sovereign.

42:1-7 –The gentleness of Messiah & His ministries of the Covenant and of healing.

50:5-8 - The Messiah's abuse before crucifixion.

52:13-15 – His appearance, redeeming work, & ultimate glorification.

53 – The suffering Messiah who would pay for sin.

61:1-3 – Christ read this passage in the temple and attributed it to Himself (Luke 4:18).

Zephaniah   625 BC

On Jerusalem	2:1-3 Opportunity for Salvation	2:4-7 On Philistia	2:8-11 On Moab & Ammon	2:12 On Ethiopia	2:13-15 On Assyria	3:1-7 On Jerusalem	3:8 On Nations	3:9-10 Of Nations	3:11-20 Of Israel
1									

Day of Wrath	Day of Restoration
1-3:8	3:9-20

Zephaniah: The Day of the Lord

Background

Zephaniah identifies himself as of the royal line of Judah – a descendant of Hezekiah (the son of Cushi, son of Gedaliah, son of Amariah, son of Hezekiah), and the dating of his ministry to the reign of Josiah king of Judah. The book of his prophecy is appropriately dated around 625 BC.

During Zephaniah's ministry King Josiah led in Judah a national revival, even being referred to as the most righteous king in Judah's history (II Kings 23:25), however it was not enough to stay the wrath of God which came just a few years after Josiah's reign.

Content

Zephaniah's prophecy focuses on the Day of the Lord (as he repeats the phrase up to thirteen times), emphasizing the two elements of that same Day: the wrath and the restoration.

In addition to Israel, the nations of Philistia, Moab, Ammon, Ethiopia, and Assyria are all judged under the coming day of wrath. But only Israel is promised an eternal restoration.

Nahum				650-612 BC

1:1-8 Character of God	1:9-14 Corruption of Ninevah	1:15-3:4 Character of Judgment	3:5-15 Capacity of Judgment	3:16-19 Certainty of Judgment
The Proclamation 1:1-14		The Explanation 1:15-3:19		
Nahum: Judgment By A Just God				

Background & Content

The author identifies himself as Nahum the Elkoshite (1:1), most likely referring to the town of Elcesei[20], which was between Jerusalem and Gaza.

Nahum is the second of three (also Jonah and Obadiah) prophets whose recorded ministries were directed toward nations other than Israel.

Titled, the oracle of Nineveh (1:1), Nahum's prophecy was directed at the capital city of the Assyrian Empire while it still maintained its strength. The city, symbolizing the entire nation, is condemned for plotting evil against the Lord (1:11), specifically the judgment comes as vengeance (1:2) for Assyria's oppression of Israel and Judah (1:15). This prophecy shows again that God will not tolerate wickedness, and in keeping His Abrahamic Covenant, evils against His people will not go unpunished (Genesis 12:3).

The prophetic judgment came upon Nineveh, just as assured, in 612 BC, as the city was destroyed completely by the Medo, Babylonian, and Scythian alliance. This destruction was so thorough that it spelled the end of the Assyrian Empire.

Appropriately, the prophecy of Nahum fits between Assyria's last era of power and oppression of Israel and Judah, and between the destruction of Nineveh in 612 BC.

Habakkuk   609 BC

Habakkuk: The Sovereignty of God	1st Petition: Why Is Wickedness Not Judged? 1:1-4
	God's Answer: Judgment Coming Via the Chaldeans 1:5-11
	2nd Petition: Why Use the Wicked To Judge Israel? 1:12-2:1
	God's Answer: The 5 Woes 2:2-20
	Prayer of Habakkuk: God is Sovereign 3

Background

The author is identified only by his name and office (1:1), and no further biographical information is given. Due to references to the Chaldeans (1:6,15) and the impending nature of their coming, it is evident that Habakkuk's writing took place shortly before the first Chaldean (or Babylonian) invasion in 605 BC, and most probably took place very shortly after King Josiah's death in 609 BC.

Content

Habakkuk asks two significant questions regarding the promises of God in relation to Israel. The dialogue between God and Habakkuk give great insight into the purposes of God.

First, Habakkuk, bemoaning Israel's unfaithfulness to the Mosaic Covenant (1:4), questions God's justice and seeming lack of intervention. God responds with an explanation that judgment would quickly and severely come at the hands of the nation He had prepared for that task: the Chaldeans. God teaches that He is not inactive in the affairs of men, nor does His plan of the ages falter.

Again, Habakkuk questions how God can use such a wicked nation as His tool to correct Israel. God responds by proclaiming five woes against the wicked, and against Babylon. God's explanation of His direction of human events is quite simple: "Let the earth be silent before Him" (2:20b). Reminiscent of Paul's explanation of the sovereignty of God (Romans 9:20-21), God's response to Habakkuk is such that the only appropriate response was one of praise and prayer.

God keeps His promises.

Jeremiah   627-586 BC

Jeremiah: Old Covenant Consequences & New Covenant Hope	Judah's Last Days 1-23	1	Appointment of Jeremiah
		2-3:10	Israel's Unfaithfulness
		3:11-4:18	Call To Repentance
		4:19-6:30	Coming Judgment
		7-9	Judgment Proclaimed
		10	The Foolishness of Idolatry
		11	The Covenant Broken
		12	Jeremiah's Prayer
		13-17	The Pride & Failures of Judah
		18-20	Persecution of Jeremiah
		21-23	Message to Kings & Prophets
	Jerusalem Under Siege 24-38	24-26:6	Prophecy Regarding Exile
		26:7-24	Persecution of Jeremiah
		27-30	Prophecies of Exile & Return
		31	The New Covenant
		32-33	Restoration Assured
		34	Judgment of Zedekiah
		35	Obedience of the Rechabites & Disobedience of Judah
		36	The Scroll of Jeremiah
		37-38	Persecution of Jeremiah
	Jerusalem Falls 39-52	39-45	Fall of Jerusalem & Jews in Egypt
		46-50	Judgment of Nations
		51	Judgment of Babylon
		52	Fall of Jerusalem & Exile

Key Promises

Background

Jeremiah identifies himself as the son of Hilkiah, of the Priests of Anathoth in Benjamin (1:1). He was both priest and prophet. And he was assisted in his writing by Baruch, who functioned as Jeremiah's secretary (36:4)

He identifies his ministry as commencing during the reign of Josiah, the righteous king of Judah, and continuing until the exile of Jerusalem. His ministry to the Southern Kingdom of Judah started early in his life, while he was still a youth (1:6), and continued for a period of over forty years.

Content

Like the prophet Isaiah, Jeremiah also intersperses historical narrative within his prophetic message, including his own imprisonment and opposition to his message (20, 26, & 32), the response of Hananiah to God's prophecy of exile (28), the reading of the Law, and Jeremiah's imprisonment under Zedekiah (36-38), the fall of Jerusalem and flight to Egypt of some Jews (39-45), and the recounting of the fall of Jerusalem (52).

Jeremiah's message to Judah was that judgment via exile was assured, and submission to the invaders was commanded (27). This was obviously an unpopular message, and Jeremiah was persecuted for it, however he had been prepared beforehand to deal with the opposition he would face (1), a reminder that God prepares His people for the tasks He gives them (Eph. 2:10).

Jeremiah 25:1-14; 29:10
The 70-Year Exile

God pronounced upon Israel, and specifically Judah, a precise seventy-year exile as consequence of breaking the Mosaic Covenant. The seventy-year period would allow the land to enjoy the Sabbath years that Israel had failed to keep while dwelling in it (Lev. 25 & 26). But after this period, Israel would be restored to her land. The initial siege of Nebuchadnezzar against Jerusalem and consequent exile took place in 605 BC, while the first return under Zerubbabel occurred in 537-536 BC, and thus the political exile was seventy years. Zechariah 1:12 seems to indicate (as of 520 BC the exile was considered by Zechariah to still be continuing) that this exile specifically referred to the destruction of the temple in 586 BC, and its restoration in 516 BC – thus encapsulating a spiritual exile.

Jeremiah 30:7
Jacob's Trouble

> Alas! For that day is great, there is none like it, and it is the time of Jacob's distress, but he will be saved from it.

Jeremiah gives a further glimpse of the far aspect of God's judgment on Israel, as well as God's primary purpose for what will be further identified by Daniel (Daniel 9) as Israel's 70th Week, and by Jesus (Matt. 24) as the Tribulation. It will be a final refining of Israel as she prepares for the 2nd Coming of her Messiah King.

Jeremiah 31:27-40
The New Covenant

This promise is of the utmost importance for God's keeping of His unconditional Covenants. The Abrahamic and Davidic Covenants both point to an eternal people and an eternal kingdom, but neither of them deals specifically with the problem of sin, that problem which would seem to render the keeping of these Covenants as impossible. Neither of those Covenants specifically address the allusion of redemption in Genesis 3:15. Neither of them specifies how eternal life is attained. The Mosaic Covenant certainly didn't either, as it simply served to magnify the failings of man and the need for redemption.

The journey of the Old Testament climaxes with this promise:

> 'Behold, days are coming', declares the Lord, 'when I will make a new covenant with the house of Israel and with the house of Judah, not like the covenant which I made with their fathers in the day I took them by the hand to bring them out of the land of Egypt, My covenant which they broke, although I was a husband to them,' declares the Lord. 'But this is the covenant I will make with the house of Israel after those days,' declares the Lord, 'I will put My law within them, and on their heart I will write it; and I will be their God and they shall be My people. And they shall not teach again each man his neighbor and each man his brother saying, 'Know the Lord,' for they shall all know Me from the least of them to the greatest of them,' declares the Lord, **'for I will forgive their iniquity, and their sin I will remember no more.'** (31:31-34)

There are five key elements revealed in the New Covenant:

1. It would be made with Israel specifically.

Again, this was a precisely aimed Covenant that would only apply to Israel.

2. It would be characterized by spiritual life and an intimate knowledge of God.

In contrast to the Mosaic Covenant, which had a national scope, this would be an individual Covenant, dealing with individual responsibility and individual knowledge of and fellowship with God, yet it would be universally effectual on all of Israel.

3. It would result in the forgiveness of the individual sins of the Israelites.

This Covenant would not simply provide a temporary atonement or covering for sin, rather it would eliminate them by virtue of forgiveness. Yet, God, in His justice would not simply sweep the sin under the rug. As pictured by the ram in the thicket at Isaac's deliverance (Gen.22), Christ would be the substitutionary Sacrifice for sin (Isaiah 53), in order that God could forgive the offenders of their sin.

4. It would include the elements of physical restoration of the nation (31:27-30; 31:38-40)

In fulfillment of the Abrahamic and Davidic Covenants, there would be a lasting people, restored to her land for eternity.

5. It would find it's ultimate fulfillment taking place after Jacob's Trouble.

The element of forgiveness of sin becomes present tense when the New Covenant is ratified by Christ in the upper room (Matt. 26:26-29), yet the national elements of physical and spiritual restoration would not become effective until the 2nd Coming of the Messiah King.

There is a sixth element that is not revealed in Jeremiah. This is the fulfillment of the Abrahamic promise that "in you all the nations of the earth shall be blessed". It is the mystery, later to be unveiled, that the Gentiles may participate in the forgiveness element of the New Covenant also (Ephesians 3:1-5). It becomes *the* promise to the church (I John 2:25).

Serving as the last prophet before and during one of the most severe periods of judgment in Israel's history, Jeremiah was used of God to bring the most profound message of hope the world could ever know. God keeps His promises.

CHAPTER V
PROMISES DELAYED
EXILE

605-536 BC - Political Exile

586-516 BC – Spiritual Exile

Prophetic Books

Lamentations	Ezekiel	Daniel

Key Promises

The Coming Kingdom ----------------------------Ezekiel 37-48
The Timeline --Daniel 9

Lamentations					586 BC

Weeping For Israel	Judgment: Thorough & Deserved	Jeremiah Laments Judgment	Jeremiah Hopes in God	Judgment Detailed	Jeremiah Prays For God's Mercy
		3:1-18	3:19-66		
1	2	3		4	5

Lamentations: Weeping for Israel

Background

The sixth book of the ketuvim is titled *e'kah* in the Hebrew, meaning literally, 'how', after the first word of the text. The Vulgate added a subtitle referring to the book as comprising "the Lamentations of Jeremiah the prophet".[21]

While the authorship is nowhere stated within the book, there is significant evidence that Jeremiah indeed penned the work, including the timeframe and nature of Jeremiah's ministry, the possible reference to the book in II Chronicles 35:25, and the agreement of Jewish tradition.

Content

The book consists of five poems (one for each chapter) in acrostic form.

The first mourns the exile (1:3) and the fall of Jerusalem from favor (1:17).

The second acknowledges the destruction is due to the anger of God (2:1).

The third is in two thematic parts, as first Jeremiah personalizes the judgment, mourning his own affliction and rejection (3:7-13), and then he rejoices just and merciful ways of the Lord (3:22-23).

The fourth recounts the horrors of the siege leading to the destruction of Jerusalem, focusing in vivid terms on the famine resulting from the siege (4:10).

The final poem is Jeremiah's prayer for mercy upon the nation and his plea for Israel's restoration.

It is notable that Jeremiah penned the following words in the midst of the greatest turmoil of his lifetime:

> The Lord's lovingkindnesses indeed never cease, for His compassions never fail. They are new every morning; Great is Thy faithfulness. (3:22-23)

Even when God's mercies were not evident in the circumstances surrounding Israel, Jeremiah takes Him at His Word, and draws powerful hope from the promises of God.

Ezekiel

593-570 BC

Ezekiel: Judgment & The Kingdom Hope	1-36:21	Visions Of Judgment	1	5th year:	Ezekiel's Visions of God

Section	Range	Subsection	Chapter	Year	Description
Ezekiel: Judgment & The Kingdom Hope	1-36:21	Visions Of Judgment	1	5th year:	Ezekiel's Visions of God
			2-3		Appointment of Ezekiel
			4-5		Judgment of Jerusalem Portrayed
			6		Idolatry Judged
			7		Wickedness Judged
			8-9	6th year:	Vision of Abomination & Judgment
			10		God's Glory Departs the Temple
			11:1-13		Leadership Judged
			11:14-25		Return From Exile Promised
			12		Exile Portrayed
			13		Judgment On False Prophets
			14:1-11		Call to Repentance For Idolatry
			14:12-15:8		Judgment & Restoration of Jerusalem
			16		God's Grace to Unfaithful Israel
			17		2 Eagles & The Vine: Consequences of Unfaithfulness
			18		Individual Responsibility
			19		Lamentation for the Princes of Israel
			20	7th year:	God's Grace to Unfaithful Israel
			21		God's swords of Judgment
			22		Israel's Wrongdoing
			23		Oholah & Oholibah: Unfaithfulness
			24	9th year:	Fall of Jerusalem: Arrival & Portrayal
			25-32	9th-12th year:	Judgment on Nations
			33:1-20		Ezekiel the Watchman
			33:21-33		Jerusalem's Fall
			34		Judgment of Shepherds & God's Care For His Sheep
			35-36:21		Judgment On Mt. Seir & Blessings on Mountains of Israel
	36:22-48:35	Visions Of Hope	36:22-38		Israel's Restoration
			37:1-14		Dry Bones: The Ingathering
			37:15-28		A United Kingdom
			38-39		Invasion & Judgment of Gog: 7 Oracles
			40-47:13	25th year:	The Kingdom Temple
			47:14-48:35		The Land of the Kingdom

Key Promise

The Coming Kingdom ----------------------------Ezekiel 37-48

Background

Ezekiel identifies himself as 'the priest, son of Buzi' (1:3). Thus like Jeremiah he filled roles as both priest and prophet. His prophetic ministry began at age thirty (1:1) in the fifth year of the exile of Jehoiachin, which took place in 597 BC. Therefore, the prophecy of Ezekiel begins in 593 BC. Ezekiel was one of the deportees of this second deportation (the first being in 605 BC and the third in 586 BC), and his visions begin near the river Chebar in Chaldea.

Ezekiel's authorship has not been questioned, even by rationalistic critics, until recently, and the modern criticisms come based on two suppositions:

1. Since the book is clearly demarked into two sections – one of judgment, and one of blessing – two authors must have been involved. This theory is as ridiculous as it sounds, and it discounts God's use of His prophets to communicate multi faceted messages - including both judgment and restoration – in many other instances.

2. Many of the prophecies (such as 11:13) seem to be written from the perspective of someone living in Judah, while Ezekiel claimed to have lived as an exile in the Chaldean territories. Again, this criticism discounts several logical explanations: first, news of events (such as 11:13) could have reached Ezekiel fairly quickly, also, God could have easily shown the prophet the events as they were happening (as He did with other prophets such as Daniel and the apostle John) – after all, the visions were supernatural to begin with.[22]

Content

God's purpose can be clearly seen, as the book is characterized by the repetition of the phrase *'then they shall know that I am the Lord'* (or a form of the phrase) some fifty times. Certainly, God sought to cause the nation to see that He was indeed the Covenant Keeping God, that He had judged Israel justly, and that He would restore Israel mercifully just as He had promised.

Ezekiel's prophecy is traced chronologically throughout the book, beginning in his 5th year of exile, as he recounts a grand vision of God, and his appointment as a prophet to the soon to be exiled peoples of Israel. His fifth year prophecies continue through chapter 7 as the thorough judgment and destruction of Jerusalem is prophesied.

Ezekiel's 6th year brings another prophecy of judgment spanning chapters 8-19, and encompassing vivid portrayals of Jerusalem's impending destruction, including God's Glory leaving the temple (10). Even amidst this judgment, God would remember His covenant with Israel even establishing a new and everlasting covenant to result in Israel's eternal restoration (16:60-63).

Chapters 20-23 cover Ezekiel's 7th year, and provide pronouncement and portrayal of God's final judgment of the nation.

The 9th year of exile brought a renewed siege of Jerusalem. After just less than six months of horror filled siege, Jerusalem was utterly destroyed (II Kings 25:1-21), and the prophecies of judgment were fulfilled. Ezekiel's prophecies shifted in focus from Israel to the nations that had afflicted them in the past, as he proclaimed judgment upon the nations in chapters 25-32.

Chapters 33-36:21 brought the conclusion of the 12th year prophecies of Ezekiel as watchman, judgment upon the leaders of Israel, judgment upon nations, and the beginning of the message of hope for Israel.

The message of restoration gains momentum in 36:22-38, as Ezekiel speaks of a physical restoration (36:24), then a spiritual restoration (36:27), and introduces the coming Kingdom.

Ezekiel 37-48
The Coming Kingdom

One of the most amazing panoramas of Biblical prophecy is found in Ezekiel 37-48. Ezekiel recounts his vision of the valley of the dry bones (ch. 37), a portrayal of the future ingathering of the nation to her land, and also speaks of the restoration of the Davidic Kingdom.

[It is worthy of note to point out that the Kingdom consists of physical restoration first, and spiritual restoration second –in stark contrast to the allegorical conclusions of replacement theology (that the church replaces Israel), which suggests spiritual domination of the church first, followed by a physical return and reign of Christ – a view inconsistent with Biblical eschatology.]

But before Israel would enjoy eternity in her restored Kingdom, there would be a confederacy of nations that would come against Israel as described in chapters 38-39: Persia (modern day Iran), Ethiopia (the Sudan), Put (a nation next to Persia), Gomer (modern day Germany), and Beth Togarmah (Armenia, possibly Turkey and Siberia). This confederacy is led by 'Gog of the land of Magog, the prince of Rosh, Meshech, and Tubal' (38:2-3).

Magog, Tubal, and Meshech are identified as sons of Japheth (Gen. 10:2), and Gog's location is said to be the 'remote parts of the north' (38:15 & 39:2). The best evidence suggests that this is a strong reference to Russia.[23]

(Some suggest plausibly that this confederacy led attack on Jerusalem will occur before the 2nd Coming of

Christ, and while this is certainly possible, it seems more likely to be the climax of Satan's final rebellion after the Millennial Kingdom, and is described in Revelation 20:8-9: Note that in both Rev.20:8-9 and Ezek.38:6 it is the fire of God which wins the victory)

Chapters 40-48 record the literal measurements of the Kingdom temple and the literal boundaries of the Kingdom land. This references the Millennial reign of Christ spoken of in Revelation 20.

In the context of the Millennial Kingdom, there is question about the purpose for the renewed sacrificial system. It must be remembered that the blood of animal sacrifices can never remit sins (Hebrews 10:4) and therefore, the Millennial system of sacrifice has nothing to do with issues of sin and forgiveness. It is also important to recognize that the promises of the Kingdom were not based on the conditional Mosaic Covenant which included animal sacrifice, but rather on the unconditional Abrahamic, Davidic, and ultimately New Covenant. The sacrifices of the Mosaic Covenant would point forward, prefiguring in memorial roughly 1400 years to the sacrifice of Christ. The sacrifices during the Millennium would point back in memorial of that same sacrifice. Each age has a memorial, whether prefiguring or remembering back to the cross of Christ. The Mosaic age had the animal sacrifices of the Mosaic Covenant. The church age has the Lord's Supper (which will also continue in the Kingdom, see Matthew 26:29). The Kingdom will have both.

The amount of time passed between Christ's sacrifice and the commencement of the Millennial Kingdom (which if it commenced seven years from now would be over 2000 years) would certainly warrant this type of memorial.

In any case, the coming of the Kingdom was assured, and the promise offered hope to repentant Jews who were now exiled from their land.

Daniel   **605-536 BC**

	1	Daniel, Hananiah, Mishael, & Azariah
	2	Nebuchadnezzar's Dream: The Great Statue: Babylon, Medo-Persia & Greece, Rome, Kingdom of God
	3	Nebuchadnezzar's Image: Shadrach, Meshach & Abadnego
	4	The Humbling of Nebuchadnezzar
	5:1-30	Belshazzar's Feast, Condemnation, & Demise
	5:31-6:28	Daniel Under Darius: The Lions Den
	7	The 4 Beasts: 4 Kings & the 10 Horn Kingdom
	8	The Ram & The Goat: Medo-Persia & Greece
	9	Daniel's Prayer & God's Response: 70 Weeks
	10	Daniel's Vision of Truth & Conflict
	11:1-39	Truth & Conflict: Rise & Fall of Kings
	11:40-12:8	The End Time
	12:9-13	Final Words to Daniel

Daniel: The Timeline of the Ages

Key Prophetic Issue

The Timeline --Daniel 9

Background

Daniel, a youth of noble blood (1:3-4), was taken captive in Nebuchadnezzar's first conquest of Jerusalem in 605 BC, and ministered there for roughly seventy years. As he completes the book, he is aged and told to prepare for death (12:13). The best date for the completion of the book is 536 BC, as his final visions occurred in the third year of the reign of Cyrus of Persia (10:1), who ruled from 539-530 BC.

Due to the amazing precision of Daniel's prophecies, critics have suggested a later date of 167 BC, citing the book's placement in the ketuvi'im rather than the nebi'im (this conclusion overlooks the fact that Daniel did not minister as a prophet as did those writers in the nebi'im, rather he was a head of state serving under the Chaldeans.).

Keil says of the book of Daniel,

> Its place in the canon among the Kethubim corresponds with the place which Daniel occupied in the kingdom of God under the Old Testament; the alleged want of references to the book and its prophecies in Zechariah and in the [apocryphal] book of Jesus Sirach is, when closely examined, not really the case: not only Jesus Sirach and Zechariah knew and understood the prophecies of Daniel, but even Ezekiel names Daniel as a bright pattern of righteousness and wisdom.[24]

There are other internal issues that have concerned critics, such as the presence of Greek-influenced terms within the text, however archaeology (particularly in the remains of Nineveh) has evidenced that Greek influence was felt even before Daniel's time.[25] Also of concern is the seeming error of Daniel 1:1 which identifies Nebuchadnezzar's invasion as being in the third year of

Jehoiakim, while Jeremiah 46:2 indicates it took place in Jehoiakim's fourth year. This is easily explained by the difference between the Jewish and Chaldean calendars, however, with Jeremiah writing from the perspective of the Jewish calendar, while Daniel wrote from the perspective of the Chaldean calendar.

The book of Daniel is difficult for some to accept, as it contains the future of the world, communicated with precision and purpose, and finds it's ultimate fulfillment in the Kingdom of Jesus Christ.

Content

Daniel begins the book with a narrative of how he came to his esteemed position, specifically by virtue of the favor and provision of God (1:9, 17-20).

In chapter 2 Daniel's ministry of 'understanding' (1:17) was applied to the dream of Nebuchadnezzar, which Daniel identified and interpreted. The dream was a vision of a great statue, the head of which was fine gold (symbolizing the first kingdom, Babylon), the breast and arms of which were silver (symbolizing Medo Persia), the belly and thighs of which were bronze (symbolizing Greece), and the legs were of iron (symbolizing Rome), with the feet partly of iron and partly of clay (symbolizing a divided Rome). The statue was crushed by an uncut stone (which symbolized the kingdom of Messiah).

Nebuchadnezzar responded favorably toward Daniel, promoting him, but did not humble himself before God, as evidenced by his construction of a golden image of himself in chapter 3. Nebuchadnezzar demanded nationwide worship of the statue, which brought about God's protection of Shadrach, Meshach, and Abednego from the fiery consequences they received for breaking this edict.

The Babylonian king temporarily humbled himself before God, but was ultimately disciplined by God in chapter 4 on account of his arrogance, after which time he humbled himself and honored the Lord.

Chapter 5 records the arrogance and debauchery of Belshazzar, and the judgment that was pronounced on him by God's handwriting on the wall.

Chapter 6, emphasizing the fulfillment of the prophecy regarding Belshazzar's demise and the ultimate conquest of the Babylonians by the Medo-Persians (5:25-28), records Daniel's service to Darius the Mede, including the account of God's protecting Daniel from the lions in the lions' den.

Chapter 7 continues Daniel's visions of the ages, as he sees a vision of four beasts, symbolizing the four kingdoms to reign before Messiah. The fourth beast (Rome) had ten horns, symbolizing ten kingdoms (divided Rome) that would arise. Another horn devoured three of the horns, and it became exceedingly great for three and a half years before it would be judged and overthrown by Messiah. This stunning vision refers to antichrist's dominance over a new restored yet divided Rome, and his ultimate defeat by Christ.

The panoramic visions continue in chapter 8: This time Daniel sees a ram with two horns (Medo-Persian) that was shattered by a goat with one conspicuous horn (Greece, led by Alexander the Great). The goat grew arrogant, and the horn was broken, and four horns came up in its place (referring to the division of Alexander's kingdom between his four generals). One of the horns grows exceedingly great, and from it comes the fourth kingdom, and the prince (another reference to antichrist) who magnifies himself, equating himself with the Lord of Hosts, and he stops sacrifice in the temple, and causes transgression for 2300 days, or six years and one hundred and ten days. This is roughly six months short of the seven-year period prophesied for the period of the tribulation, and it most likely takes into account the time necessary to set up the sacrificial system at the beginning of the seven-year period.[26]

Daniel 9
The Timeline: Daniel's 70 Weeks

Chapter 9 finds Daniel examining the prophet Jeremiah's declarations of a seventy-year exile (Jeremiah 25:14, 29:10), and responding humbly to the Lord in prayer, as the time of the exile was drawing to a close. The personal humility that Daniel demonstrates in his prayer is exemplary. Ezekiel presents him as one of three most righteous men in Scripture (Ezekiel 14:14,20).

God holds Daniel in such high regard that before he even concludes his prayer, the angel Gabriel is sent to provide an answer to his prayer. Gabriel speaks to Daniel regarding the timeline of future events:

> Seventy weeks have been decreed for your people and your holy city, to finish the transgression, to make an end of sin, to make atonement for iniquity, to bring in everlasting righteousness, to seal up vision and prophecy, and to anoint the most holy place. (9:24)

The seventy weeks is literally seventy 'sevens' (heptamades in the Greek), and refers to seventy Sabbaths of years (Leviticus 25:8), or 490 years.
There are two elements of purpose, with 6 specific results:

A. Dealing with sin
>   1. to finish the transgression
>   2. to make an end of sin
>   3. to make atonement for iniquity (Christ at the cross)

B. Dealing with righteousness
>   4. to bring in everlasting righteousness (Jer. 23:5-6; 31)
>   5. to seal up vision and prophecy – *to seal* in the sense of royal authentication, fulfilling God's plan

6. to anoint the most holy – either referring to the temple or the Messiah

So you are to know and discern that from the issuing of a decree to restore and rebuild Jerusalem until Messiah the Prince there will be seven weeks and sixty two weeks; it will be built again, with plaza and moat, even in times of distress. (9:25)

The first seven weeks (49 years) probably references the remaining years of Old Testament prophetic ministry after the decree of King Artaxerxes in Nehemiah 2:1-6 (the only decree pertaining to the actual city)[27], while the following sixty-two covers the inter-testamental period (434 years), which would include the 400 years of silence (Amos 8:11).

Prophetic Math

This adds up to a total of 483 years of 360-day years (according to the Jewish lunar calendar). According to the sun calendar, years are made up of 365 days. The lunar calendar would add a 13th month to make up the difference when enough days had accumulated, but this addition is not characteristic of Biblical prophecy (see Rev. 11:2,3; 12:6; 13:5), so five days per year must be subtracted to fit into the lunar calendar. Five days times 483 years equals 2415 extra days, or roughly 6 2/3 years.

Here is the formula: 445 BC + 483 years = 38 AD – 6years (for the lunar calendar adjustment) = 32 AD, which would complete the seven and sixty-two weeks of years.

Then after the sixty-two weeks the Messiah will be cut off and have nothing, and the people of the prince who is to come will destroy the city and the sanctuary. And its end will come with a

> flood; even to the end there will be war; desolations are determined. (9:26)

There is historical consensus that Christ was crucified in 33 AD (fulfilling the first part of this prophecy), and that Rome destroyed Jerusalem in 70 AD (fulfilling the second). Thus the first 483 years of the 490-year schedule is completed.

> And he will make a firm covenant with the many for one week, but in the middle of the week he will put a stop to sacrifice and grain offering; and on the wing of abominations will come one who makes desolate, even until a complete destruction, one that is decreed is poured out on the one who makes desolate. (9:27)

The people who destroyed Jerusalem were Rome, and therefore the prince would be a Roman prince, presiding over the ten-kingdom confederacy of Rome. He will make a seven-year covenant, which he will break in the middle of its term, bringing about extreme destruction and ultimately being destroyed himself. This clearly describes the activity of antichrist during the tribulation period immediately prior to the 2nd coming of Messiah.

The final seven-year period of this prophecy commences with the prince's covenant, so the timeline has paused for some time, awaiting his arrival on the scene. The purpose for this gap is later explained in Romans 9-11.

Imagine Daniel's amazement. He had sought the Lord for an end to the exile, and God provided him with the timeline to the ultimate restoration of Jerusalem.

Conclusion

Daniel's visions continue in chapter 10, as he sees a terrifying vision, the details of which he does not record.

The prophecy of chapter 11 describes later events of Persia and Greece with such detail and precision that liberal critics accuse the author of writing after the events had taken place.

Chapter 12 concludes Daniel's visions with a message of encouragement from Michael the archangel, as he describes the future salvation and restoration of God's people. Daniel asks how long until the wonders are completed, and Michael responds by saying "a time, times, and a half a time" (12:7), referring to the latter three and a half years of the tribulation. This is the time of great tribulation described in Matthew 24.

Daniel seeks hope in the Lord at the outset of chapter 9. God's response provides the purpose for the revelation of His plan. His Eschatological plan gives us hope, as it reminds us that He is sovereignly in control of all earthly events, and His plan is being fulfilled to the letter. His promises are true, and we can trust in Him, for He is our Hope.

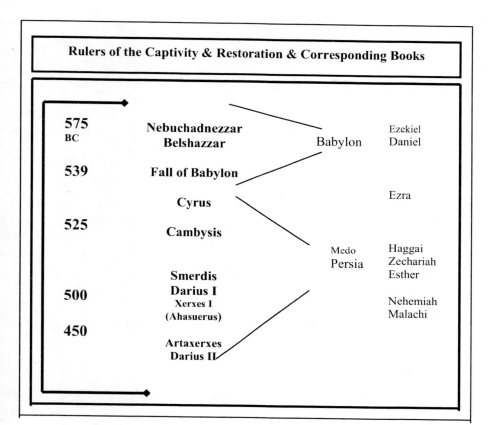

Rulers of the Captivity & Restoration & Corresponding Books

575 BC	**Nebuchadnezzar** **Belshazzar**	Babylon	Ezekiel Daniel
539	**Fall of Babylon**		
	Cyrus		Ezra
525	**Cambysis**		
500	**Smerdis** **Darius I** Xerxes I (Ahasuerus)	Medo Persia	Haggai Zechariah Esther Nehemiah Malachi
450	**Artaxerxes** **Darius II**		

CHAPTER VI

PROMISES KEPT
RETURN & RESTORATION

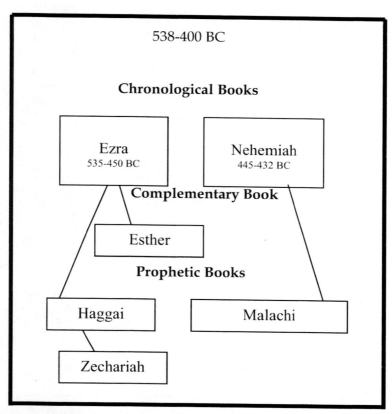

Key Fulfillment

Exile Ended: Completion of the Temple --------Ezra 6:13-15

Key Promise

The Forerunner, Messiah, & Judgment ---------Malachi 3:1-6

Ezra			538-450 BC

Ezra: Spiritual Restoration – The Temple	1st Return: Zerubbabel	1	Cyrus Decree For Temple Restoration
		2	Census of the Returning Exiles
		3:1-7	Festivals & Sacrifices Resumed
		3:8-13	Temple Restoration Begun
		4:1-16	Temple Restoration Opposed: Shimshei & Rehum
		4:17-24	Artexerxes Decree to Cease Temple Restoration
	1-6	5	Temple Restoration Resumed Despite Opposition
		6:1-13	Darius Sanctions Temple Completion
		6:14-22	Temple Completed, Dedicated, & Utilized
	2nd Return: Ezra	7	Artaxerxes Decrees Ezra's Return
		8:1-20	Census of the Returning Exiles
		8:21-36	God Provides a Safe Return
		9	Israel's Sin of Intermarriage
	7-10	10:1-17	Israel's Restitution
		10:18-44	Census of Those Who Intermarried

Key Fulfillment

Exile Ended: Completion of the Temple --------Ezra 6:13-15

Background

Originally combined with Nehemiah in the Hebrew canon, Ezra has traditionally been regarded as the author, utilizing the writings of Nehemiah, which formed the latter section of the combined books. Division of the two books was first made in the Latin Vulgate, and has since become common.

Ezra is identified as a descendant of the priestly line of Aaron (7:1-3), and as a scribe skilled in the Law (7:6).

The book covers historical events occurring between the years 538-450 BC, and as he was probably the author of the Chronicles, they were most likely completed during this timeframe as well.

Summary

Chapters 1-6 recounts the first return of Israel from exile under Zerubbabel in 537-536 BC, numberings of those exiles returning, and the completion of the restoring of the temple in 516 BC. This completed the seventy-year exile as prophesied in Jeremiah (25:14; 29:10), as the temple restoration was completed precisely seventy years after it was destroyed (in 586 BC).

Chapters 7-10 record the second return, this time under Ezra, in 458 BC. This return focused on the spiritual restoration of the exiled nation, as they recommitted themselves to obedience to God.

The book of Ezra provides further evidence of God's faithfulness to His promise as the history of Israel continued to unfold.

Haggai   520 BC

1st Word					2nd Word	3rd Word	4th Word
1:1-4 Problem: Disobedience – Temple Neglected	1:5-6 Result: Judgment – Israel Neglected	1:7-8 Command: Obedience – Build Temple	1:9-11 Alternative: Judgment – Neglect of Israel	1:12-15 Obedience: Temple Construction Begun	2:1-9 The Obedient Have Hope – God Is Faithful	2:10-19 The Obedient Are Holy – Israel Must Be Holy	2:20-23 The Obedient Are Blessed – Blessing of Zerubbabel

Haggai: Word of Renewed Obedience

Background

The author is identified as Haggai the prophet (1:1). His ministry is linked with that of Zechariah (Ezra 5:1), although Haggai's slightly predated Zechariah's by about two months (Hag. 1:1, Zech 1:1). The dating of his writing is clear, as Haggai postscripts each of the four sections of the book. A date of 520 BC is ascribed.

Content

The returning exiles were encountering significant opposition in their attempts to rebuild the temple, and the work had come to a stop (Ezra 4).

Chapter 1 recounts the Lord's call to continue the temple effort, and the obedience of Haggai and Zerubbabel.

Less than two months later, another word of the Lord came to Haggai, this one a message of encouragement based on the faithfulness of God.

Two months later, a third word of the Lord came to Haggai, this time with a call to purity and a promise of blessing.

And finally, on that same day, the Lord gave Haggai a message of future blessing for the obedient Zerubbabel.

The obedience of Haggai, Zerubbabel, and the people resulted in the completion of the temple – on God's timetable – in 516 BC.

Zechariah   520-518 BC

Zechariah: Israel's Hope of Redemption	Visions 1-6	1:1-3	Admonition to Repentance
		1:4-6	Example of the Fathers
		1:7-11	Four Horses Patrolling the Earth
		1:12-17	Restoration of Israel Coming
		1:18-21	4 Horns & 4 Craftsmen
		2	Restoration of Jerusalem Coming
		3	Joshua the High Priest
		4	Golden Lampstand & 2 Olive Trees
		5:1-4	The Scroll
		5:5-11	The Ephah
		6:1-8	Four Chariots of Patrol
		6:9-15	Offering for the Crown
	Words 7-8	7	Inquiry of Bethel & Call to Obedience
		8	Restoration of Israel Coming
	Burdens 9-14	9:1-7	Judgment on Nations
		9:8-11:3	Future Deliverance of Israel
		11:4-17	The Doomed Flock & The Worthless Shepherd
		12:1-9	War & Defense of Jerusalem
		12:10-14	Israel Mourns Her Messiah
		13	Judgment of False Prophets
		14:1-8	The Coming of the Lord
		14:9-11	The Kingdom of the Lord
		14:12-21	Judgment on Nations

Background

The author identifies himself as Zechariah the prophet, the son of Berechiah, the son of Iddo (1:1). His ministry to the returned exiles began two months after that of Haggai (Hag. 1:1, Zech 1:1), and it continued for at least two years, demarking the prophecy from 520-518 BC (although some suggest a slightly later completion date of 480 BC, due to the mention of Greece in 9:13. this is a possibility, but certainly not a necessity).

Content

Zechariah's prophecy is divided into three sections: visions, words, and burdens.

The visions are found in chapters 1-6, as God shows Zechariah visions of the restoration and blessing of Jerusalem.

Two years later, the word of the Lord came to Zechariah regarding an inquiry of the men of Bethel regarding true worship, a call to obedience, and the coming prosperity of Israel.

Finally, are the burdens, or oracles, regarding judgment on nations, restoration and future uniting of Israel (9-10). The burden of chapter 11 includes a judgment on the doomed flock and a foolish shepherd. This prophecy interestingly mentions thirty shekels of silver, alluding to the price the 'flock' placed on the Good Shepherd (Zech 11:12-13; Matt. 26:15; 27:3-10).

The burden of chapter 12 includes a reference to God's pouring out of His Spirit, that Israel may weep for the Messiah they have pierced (12:10-11). As a result, the false prophets are judged (chapter 13) for leading the people away from Messiah, yet God will ultimately defend Jerusalem, defeat her enemies, and rule all the earth as the Faithful King (chapter 14).

Esther

Esther: God Protects His Covenant People	1:1-9	King Ahasuerus' Banquet
	1:10-22	Queen Vashti's Deposing
	2:1-20	Queen Vashti's Replacement: Esther (Hadasseh)
	2:21-23	Mordecai Uncovers An Assassination Plot
	3	Haman's Plot & Edict To Destroy the Jews
	4:1-3	Mordicai Uncovers Haman's Plot
	4:4-17	Esther's Intercession
	5:1-8	Esther's Banquet
	5:9-14	Haman's Hatred of Mordecai
	6:1-9	Ahasuerus Remembers Mordecai
	6:10-14	Haman's Humiliation & Mordecai's Exaltation
	7	Esther's Petition & Haman's Demise
	8:1-7	Mordecai Honored
	8:8-17	Ahasuerus' Decree: Self-Defense For the Jews
	9:1-18	The Jews Are Victorious
	9:19-32	The Jews Remember: The Feast of Purim
	10	The Greatness of Mordecai

Background

The authorship of Esther is unknown, although Mordecai seems the most probable author[28], with Nehemiah being another possibility. The book was written sometime shortly after 473 BC, which was the year the Feast of Purim was established in remembrance of God's protection of Israel[29].

Some have doubted the authenticity of the book due to its lack of a single mention of God, but the thematic elements of Esther strongly emphasize God's sovereign protection of His covenant people.

Summary

In the reign of Ahasuerus (elsewhere identified as Artaxerxes I), Queen Vashti rejects an inappropriate command to appear before the king and his guests (1:10-12). The king is angered and ultimately replaces her with a lovely Jewish woman named Esther (Hadasseh), who had managed to keep her heritage a secret from the king (2:20). During that time Mordecai, Esther's cousin, uncovered a plot, and saved the king's life, and while his act was recorded in the records, he received no reward (2:21-23).

Later, one of the king's royal officials, named Haman, was angered by Mordecai's refusal to bow down before him. This led Haman to create an edict for the destruction of the Jews (3). Esther learns of the plot, and plans a banquet to present her case to the king (4-5). In the meantime, Haman builds a gallows upon which to have ~~Haman~~ [Mordecai] hung, but the king, after reading the account of how Mordecai saved the king's life determines to honor Mordecai and requires Haman to publicly honor Mordecai (6). Esther informs the king of her heritage and Haman's plot against the Jews, resulting in Haman's execution upon the gallows he built for Mordecai (7).

The king then honors Mordecai, and gives provision for the Jews to defend themselves (8). Upon mounting a successful defense, the Jews instituted the Feast of Purim (after the *pur*, or lot that Haman cast for the destruction of the Jews in 3:7).

The book of Esther gives the miraculous account of God's provision for the survival of His people. In order for Him to keep His word, the Jews must survive. The book acknowledges Sovereign control and purpose in human events, as evidenced by Mordecai's statement to Esther: "And who knows whether you have attained royalty for such a time as this?" (4:14)

God will protect His people, and will judge those who come against them, just as He promised (Gen. 12:3).

Nehemiah   445-433 BC

Nehemiah: Political Restoration - Jerusalem	Walls Restored	1-7:4	1 — Nehemiah's Prayer
			2:1-8 — Artaxerxes Sanctions Nehemiah's Return
			2:9-20 — Sanballat's Opposition
			3 — Builders of the Wall
			4:1-8 — Sanballat's Opposition
			4:9-23 — Opposition Thwarted
			5:1-13 — Usury Stopped
			5:14-19 — Nehemiah's Leadership
			6:1-14 — Opposition: Sanballat, Tobiah, & Geshem
			6:15-7:4 — Wall Completed Despite Opposition
	Commitment Restored	7:5-13:31	7:5-73 — Census of the 1st Return
			8:1-12 — Remembrance & Convocation: Ezra & Nehemiah
			8:13-18 — Israel Observes the Feast of Booths
			9:1-37 — Israel Repents
			9:38-10:39 — Israel's Covenant: Commitment to the Law & Temple
			11:1-19 — Leaders in Jerusalem
			11:20-36 — Cities of Judah, Benjamin, & The Levites
			12:1-26 — Priests & Levites of the 1st Return
			12:27-30 — Dedication of the Wall of Jerusalem
			12:31-43 — The Choirs of Jerusalem
			12:44-47 — Portions For Singers, Levites, & Sons of Aaron
			13 — Israel's Preparation & Purification

Background

Originally united with Ezra as one book in the Hebrew canon, the Vulgate separated the two, the latter of which was authored by Nehemiah, the son of Hacaliah (1:1). He served as governor for the returned exiles from 445-433 BC (5:14).

The events of Nehemiah begin in 445 BC (2:1) and conclude twelve years later (13:6).

Summary

Chapters 1-7:4 recount the restoration of the wall of Jerusalem, despite opposition from Sanballat and others. This completes the physical and political restoration from exile.

Chapter 7:5-13:31 recount the restoration of the returned exiles' commitment to God, as proper worship is restored.

Nehemiah is chronologically the final historical book of the Old Testament. The book focuses on Israel's return and political restoration from exile. God had kept His promise to deliver a remnant from the exile in Babylon, and He would keep His other promises relating to the future Kingdom of Israel. But first would come one final prophetic messenger (Malachi), who would look to the coming preparations for Messiah, and then would come the years of silence (Amos 8:11), the famine for new revelation during the inter-testamental period.

Malachi   450-400 BC

Malachi: Israel's Failures & Future Hope	1:1-5 God's Plan For Jacob & Esau
	1:6-2:9 Sin & Judgment of the Priests
	2:10-16 Unfaithfulness of Israel
	2:17-3:6 Coming Justice
	3:7 Israel's Turning Away
	3:8-12 Israel's Failure in Tithing
	3:13-15 Israel's Arrogance
	3:16-18 Israel's Remembrance
	4 Israel's Future & The Day of the Lord

Key Promise

The Forerunner, The Messiah, & Judgment ----Malachi 3:1-6

Background

The final prophetic messenger of the Old Testament identifies himself simply as Malachi (1:1).

Archer lists the evidence for a mid-fifth century authorship:

> (1) the temple had already been rebuilt and Mosaic sacrifice reinstituted (1:7, 10;3:10)…(3) The sins which Malachi denounces are the same as those Nehemiah had to correct during his second term, namely (a) priestly laxity (1:6; Neh. 13:4-9), (b) neglect of tithes, to the impoverishment of the Levites (3:7-12; cf. Neh 13:10-13), (c) much intermarriage with foreign women (2:10-16; cf. Neh. 13:23-28). It is reasonable to assume that Malachi had already protested against these abuses in the years just preceding Nehemiah's return; hence a fair estimate would be about 435 BC.[30]

Content

Contradicting the newfound commitment Israel proclaimed in the latter times of Nehemiah, Israel had failed to turn completely from the very errors she repented of during Nehemiah's day. Particular judgments and warnings came to the priests for their unfaithfulness (1:6-2:9), and to the people for their failures in attending to the matters of God's house: specifically, their failure to tithe (3:8-12). But as was characteristic of God in His mercy, against the backdrop of discipline appeared the promise of future hope.

Malachi 3:1-6
The Forerunner, Messiah, & Judgment

The first promise is of a coming messenger (3:1) who would prepare the way for Messiah. Christ ascribes this role to John the Baptist (Matt. 11:10).

The second is of the coming Messiah, who would sit as judge (3:2-4).

The third is of certain judgment and refining that Messiah would bring (3:5-6).

Israel had been through much in the Old Testament years. God had kept or further advanced every promise He had made, and now, as Israel looked forward to 400 years without new revelation from God, they had the assurance of hope, the promise of a forerunner who would announce Messiah. God keeps His promises.

CHAPTER VII
PROMISES DISTINGUISHED
ISRAEL & THE CHURCH

Israel: The Eternal **Promises**

Genesis 12:1-3 - Abrahamic Covenant
Deuteronomy 30:1-10 - Land Covenant
II Samuel 7:8-17 - Davidic Covenant
Jeremiah 31:27-40 - New Covenant

EARTHLY

Daniel 9 - The 70 Weeks of Israel Prophecied
Matthew 12 - Israel rejects her Messiah

Romans 9-11

The Church: **The** Eternal Promise

Veiled Allusion

Genesis 12:3c - Blessing to the nations
Jeremiah 31:34b - Forgiveness of sin
Joel 2:28 - Holy Spirit predicted
John 16 - Holy Spirit promised

Direct Revelation

Matthew 16:13-20 - First prophecy of the church
Acts 2 - Birth of the church
Ephesians 1-3,5 - The mystery of the church
Galatians 3-4 - The economy of the church
I John 2:25 - The promise defined
Revelation 1-3 - The conclusion of the church
I Thessalonians 4:13-18 - the rapture of the church

HEAVENLY

Revelation 4-18 - Jacob's Trouble:
The Tribulation (Daniel's 70th
week)

Revelation 19 - The King Comes

Revelation 20 - The Kingdom
Revelation 21-22 - Eternity

(church in heaven)

Revelation 19 - Christ returns
with His bride
Revelation 20 - The Kingdom
Revelation 21-22 - Eternity

Hermeneutics & Eschatology

There have historically been primarily two schools of Biblical interpretation, (1) the allegorical, and (2) the literal. Dating back to Philo (Jewish philosopher at Alexandria during the time of Christ), Origen (late 2nd century church leader), and Augustine (late 4th – early 5th century church leader), the church allegorized that which it did not understand.

Covenant Theology (which acknowledges only two covenants – that of works, made with Israel, and violated by Israel, therefore requiring replacement, and that of grace, made with the church) sprung from this method and flourishes today. There are two basic tenets of the allegorical method:

1. All prophecy is to be interpreted allegorically
2. Israel has therefore been replaced in the plan of God.

The second group of interpreters hold to a literal interpretation of scripture, which leads to a dispensational view of God's plan, summarized by the following:

> Dispensationalism is that system of theology which: views the world as a household run by God. In this household-world God is dispensing or administering its affairs according to His own will in various stages of revelation in the process of time. These various stages mark off the distinguishably different economies in the outworking of His total purpose, and these economies are the dispensations.[31]

The presupposition of the allegorical method is that God does not have plans for Israel's physical blessing in the future, due to Israel's rejection of her Messiah. To those who hold to this presupposition (as Philo, Origen, and Augustine did), the allegorical method is required, for a literal method would result in a dramatically different understanding. The interpretation of the allegorical method and Covenant Theology is that Israel is finished as a chosen vessel of God. She had her chance and failed, and now it is the church's turn, and since the gates of hell shall not prevail against her, she shall not suffer the same fate as Israel did. Rather she shall endure faithfully to the end, prevailing over her enemies. Under this presupposition, God's calling of Israel is not irrevocable (as Romans 11 declares it to be).

The logical conclusion of replacement theology is that since the church replaces Israel, she has the same authority God gave Israel, and now the church can use any means necessary to prevail throughout the world. History has witnessed this error in action with the Crusades, The Inquisition, and to some extent, even the Holocaust. Anti-Semitism in the church has come from replacement theology, Covenant theology and the allegorical method.

There are three groups of Covenant Theologians - the premillennial, the postmillennial, and the amillennial - each named for their interpretation of the eschatological event of Christ's Second Coming.

The Covenant Premillennial (Christ returns before the millennium) is perhaps closest to the Dispensationalist, in that he believes in a kingdom of God on earth after the second coming of Christ, yet he differs in that he believes the focus will be on the church, and that Israel will be excluded as a national entity.

The Covenant Postmillennial (Christ returns after the kingdom starts) believes in a kingdom on earth which is initiated by the church, not Christ. Israel is not nationally included.

The Covenant Amillennial (no millennium) believes that there is no literal kingdom but rather a spiritual kingdom in the hearts of believers, and of course, as a nation Israel is excluded.

The Dispensationalist takes quite the opposite view as that of the Covenant Theologian. The literal interpretation of Scripture brings about the conclusion that God is not at all finished with Israel, but rather He has only temporarily set the nation aside, in order that the gentiles might be saved as well. This conclusion is arrived at by allowing the text to speak for itself.

Because of the literal method, the Dispensationalist universally recognizes the premillennial return of Christ, and generally regards a pretribulational rapture of the church.

Paul speaks plainly of the state of Israel:

> I say then God has not rejected His people, has He? May it never be! (Rom. 11:1)

It is clear that the New Testament does not intend a replacement of Israel.

> Much confusion exists because of the failure to carefully define, distinguish, and compare the church and the kingdom. Based on Augustine's City of God, the equation of the church and the kingdom resulted in the absolute authority of the church on earth. Postmillennialism builds the earthly kingdom on the growth and success of the church. The mistaken concept of theonomy sees the church's mission as establishing the Old Testament Law of God in the kingdoms of the world today.[32]

Dispensational theology acknowledges the literal, eternal, and unconditional aspects of the covenants God made with Israel, and interprets their fulfillments accordingly. This can be the only logic conclusion of a literal interpretation of Scripture.

The Dispensations: Number & Purpose

12 Dispensations: *Doxological*	7 Dispensations: *Soteriological*	3 Dispensations: *Kingdom*
1. Planning Eternity Past Jn. 17:24; Eph. 1:4; 1 Pet. 1:20		
2. Prelude Innocence of Man Gen. 1:1-3:5	**1. Innocence** Gen. 1:3-3:6	
3. Plight Failure of Man Gen. 3:6-6:7	**2. Conscience** Gen. 3:7-8:14	**1. Preparation** beginning in Gen. 3:15
4. Preservation & Provision Common Grace & Human Government Gen. 6:8-11:9	**3. Government** Gen. 8:15-11:9	
5. Promises Pronounced Gen. 11:10-Ex. 18:27	**4. Promise** Gen. 11:10-Ex. 18:27	
6. Prerequisite Portrayed The Broken Covenant: The Tutor Ex. 19:1-Mal. 4:6 (Gal. 3:24-25)	**5. Law** Ex. 19:1-Jn. 14:30	
7. Promises Proffered The Kingdom Offered Mt. 1:1-12:45		
8. Postponement & Propitiation The Kingdom Postponed & New Covenant Ratified Mt. 12:46-Acts 1:26		
9. Participation The Church Age Acts 2:1- Rev. 3:22	**6. Grace** Acts 2:1 – Rev. 19:21	**2. Participation** beginning in Acts 2
10. Purification The Tribulation, Jacob's Trouble Rev. 4:1-19:10		
11. Promises Performed The Kingdom Initiated Rev. 19:11- 20:6	**7. Millennium** Rev. 20:1-5	**3. Consummation** beginning in Rev. 19
12. Postscript Eternity Future Rev. 20:7 – 22:21		

Dispensational Distinctions

In order to fully grasp the Promises of God, it is important to understand the dispensational distinction between Israel and the church. Misidentifying the roles which God has for Israel and those He has for the church results in an inability to understand God's plan of the ages and as a result, His character.

The two (Israel and the church) are neither one in identity, nor are they one in purpose. Ultimately, of course, the chief end of man is indeed to glorify God, however God clearly uses different people in different ways to bring glory to Himself. In regards to the distinction of Israel and the church, Chafer says,

> Apart from the right understanding of this subject there can be no conception of the heavenly purpose of God in and through the Church in contrast to His earthly purpose in Israel, no conception of the divine purpose in the present age, no basis for a true evaluation of all those new realities and relationships which were made possible and established through the death and resurrection of Christ, no worthy comprehension of the present ministries of the Spirit of God, and no sufficient basis of appeal for the God-honoring life and service of the believer.[33]

In Chafer's estimation, without understanding this distinction, we cannot begin to comprehend, in essence, what Paul calls "every spiritual blessing" (Ephesians 1:3) with which the church has been blessed in Christ. The scope of this distinction far transcends even eschatological issues, for certainly, *this distinction is pivotal in understanding the fullness of Biblical theology.*

Pentecost recognizes God's covenants with Israel as the building blocks of eschatology:

> The covenants contained in the Scriptures are of primary importance to the interpreter of the Word and to the student of eschatology. God's eschatological program is determined and prescribed by these covenants and one's eschatological system is determined and limited by the interpretation of them. These covenants must be studied diligently as the basis of Biblical eschatology.[34]

And again, Pentecost observes,

> Chafer has set forth twenty four contrasts between Israel and the church which show us conclusively that these two groups can not be united into one, but that they must be distinguished as two separate entities with whom God is dealing in a special program...[from Chafer, Systematic Theology, Vol IV, p. 47-53]...These contrasts may be outlined as follows:(1) The extent of Biblical revelation: Israel - nearly four fifths of the Bible; Church - about one fifth. (2) The divine purpose: Israel - the earthly promises of the covenants; Church - the heavenly promises in the gospel. (3) The seed of Abraham: Israel - the physical seed, of whom some become a spiritual seed; Church - a spiritual seed. (4) Birth: Israel - physical birth that produces a relationship; Church - spiritual birth that brings relationship. (5) Headship: Israel - Abraham; Church - Christ. (6) Covenants: Israel - Abrahamic and all the following covenants; Church - indirectly related to the Abrahamic and new covenants; (7) Nationality: Israel - one nation; Church - from all nations. (8) Divine dealing: Israel - national and individual; Church - individual only. (9) Dispensations: Israel - seen in all ages from Abraham; Church - seen only in the present age. (10) Ministry: Israel - no missionary activity and no gospel to preach; Church

- a commission to fulfill. (11) The death of Christ: Israel - guilty nationally, to be saved by it; Church - perfectly saved by it now. (12) The Father: Israel - by a peculiar relationship God was Father to the nation; Church - we are related individually to God as Father. 13) Christ: Israel - Messiah, Immanuel, King; Church - Saviour, Lord, Bridegroom, Head. (14) The Holy Spirit: Israel - Came upon some temporarily; Church - the indwelling Holy Spirit. (17) Two farewell discourses: Israel - Olivet Discourse; Church - Upper room Discourse. (18) The promise of Christ's return: Israel - in power and glory for judgment; Church - to receive us unto Himself. (19) Position: Israel - a servant; Church - members of the family. (20) Christ's earthly reign: Israel - subjects; Church - co-reigners. (21) Priesthood: Israel - had a priesthood; Church - is a priesthood. (22) Marriage: Israel - unfaithful wife; Church - bride. (23) Judgments: Israel - must face judgment; Church - delivered from judgments. (24) Positions in eternity: Israel - spirits of just men made perfect in the new earth; Church - church of the firstborn in the new heavens. These clear contrasts, which show the distinction between Israel and the church, make it impossible to identify the two in one program, which it is necessary to do if the church goes through the seventieth week. These distinctions give further support to the pretribulation rapture position.[35]

The first eleven chapters of Genesis present God's dealings with early mankind in general. It was not until the twelfth chapter that we see Him working through the seed of one particular man.Genesis 12:1-3 is assuredly the key to the unfolding of God's plan for mankind.Throughout the pages of Scripture, and through the dawning of many eras, there is a tie that binds history together. In Genesis 12, it is recorded that God chose Abraham to be the recipient of magnificent blessing. Here God makes specific promises to the physical seed of Abraham. The unfolding of these promises is the unified theme of all of Scripture, thus, here, if you will, is the outline of Scripture found.

In regard to the distinctions between Israel and the church, Pentecost explains the importance of properly understanding this covenant:

> When [the] particulars are analyzed it will be seen that certain individual promises were given to Abraham, certain national promises respecting the nation of Israel, of which he was the father, were given to him, and certain universal blessings that encompassed all nations were given to him...In the development of this covenant it is of utmost importance to keep the different areas in which promise was made clearly in mind, for if the things covenanted in one area are transferred to another area only confusion will result in the subsequent interpretation.   Personal promises may not be transferred to the nation and promises to Israel may not be transferred to the Gentiles.[36]

The promises for Abraham's seed are somewhat general, there are no details included here in regard to the specific nature of these promises, but they are clearly elaborated on in further Scriptures. Abraham would be a great nation, but how?

Deuteronomy 30:1-10 records the next eternal covenant with Israel, the physical seed of Abraham.

> So it shall be when all of these things have come upon you, the blessings and the curse which I have set before you, and you call them to mind in all the nations where the Lord has banished you, and you return to the Lord your God and obey Him with all your heart and soul according to all that I command you today, you and your sons, then the Lord your God will restore you from captivity, and have compassion on you, and will gather you again from all the peoples where the Lord your God has

scattered you. If your outcasts are at the ends of the earth, from there the Lord your God will gather you, and from there He will bring you back And the Lord your God will bring you into the land which your fathers possessed, and you shall possess it; and He will prosper you and multiply you more than you fathers. Moreover the Lord your God will circumcise your heart and the heart of your descendants, to love the Lord your God with all your heart and with all your soul, in order that you may live. And the Lord your God will inflict these curses on your enemies and on those who hate you, who persecuted you. And you shall again obey the Lord, and observe all His commandments which I command you today.

Then the Lord your God will prosper you abundantly in all the work of your hand, in the offspring of your cattle and in the produce of your ground, for the Lord will again rejoice over you for good, just as He rejoiced over your fathers; if you obey the Lord your God to keep His commandments and His statutes, which are written in the book of the Law, if you turn to the Lord your God with all your heart and all your soul. (30:1-10)

Here even the promises of Gen. 12 are expanded. Israel would fail to keep the conditional Mosaic Covenant (Ex. 20, etc.), and would be cast out of her land, but the rejection would not continue forever, for Israel would one day be restored by God into the land which He gave to her. When Israel should return this time, not only would she dwell in the land forever, but there would also be a spiritual restoration of all Israel from that point on.

Some would suggest that the fulfillment of this promise can be found in the narratives of Ezra and Nehemiah - Israel's return from exile, and restoration both to her land and to her God, but this is clearly not the case.

This return, for Israel, would be from even "the ends of the earth". This could hardly be described as Israel's return from exile in Babylon.

Also, the spiritual restoration that is to come with the physical return has never been fulfilled. The spiritual return under Ezra and Nehemiah was temporary and short lived, while the restoration here is for "you and your descendants" - generation after generation.

Thus, unquestionably, there is a still yet future promise for Israel's physical and spiritual restoration. But even the details of this restoration - at the time of Moses - were still quite vague. The fullness as of yet still had not been revealed. Pentecost again profoundly summarizes:

> From the original statement of the provisions of this covenant, it is easy to see that, on the basis of a literal fulfillment, Israel must be converted as a nation, must be regathered from her worldwide dispersion, must be installed in her land, which she is made to possess, must witness the judgment of her enemies, and must receive the material blessings vouchsafed for her. This covenant, then, is seen to have a wide influence on our eschatological expectation. Since these things have never been fulfilled, and an eternal and unconditional covenant demands a fulfillment, we must provide for just such a program in our outline of future events.[37]

In II Samuel, there is yet another expansion of the Abrahamic promises, as God makes His covenant with David. (II Samuel 7)

Once again, Israel is promised a permanent physical restoration to her land, but now we find that it will be through the line of David that the leadership will come. And that leadership will be an eternal kingdom with an eternal king. Of course the passage speaks specifically of Solomon, David's son, but the phrase "your throne shall be established forever" speaks of something much grander than the reign of Solomon. This is an eternal promise of an eternal king who would come from the very line of David.

Shortly after this period in Israel's history, in which these words to David were declared, Israel was exiled from her land. She did return 70 years later, but there was never a complete physical restoration, there was never a complete spiritual restoration, and there was never again a king in Israel - even to this very day.

The promises are either false, or else they are still yet future.

> Because of an anticipated future literal fulfillment, certain facts present themselves concerning Israel's future. (1) First of all, Israel must be preserved as a nation...(2) Israel must have a national existence, and be brought back into the land of her inheritance. Since David's kingdom had definite geographical boundaries and those boundaries were made a feature of the promise to David concerning his son's reign, the land must be given to this nation as the site of their national homeland. (3) David's son, the Lord Jesus Christ, must return to the earth, bodily and literally, in order to reign over David's covenanted kingdom. The allegation that Christ is seated on the Father's throne reigning over a spiritual kingdom, the church, simply does not fulfill the promises of the covenant.

(4) A literal earthly kingdom must be constituted over which the returned Messiah reigns...(5) this kingdom must become an eternal kingdom. Since the "throne", "house", and kingdom were all promised to David in perpetuity, there must be no end to Messiah's reign over David's kingdom from David's throne.[38]

Deuteronomy 30 gives the promise of an eternal multitude, an eternal dwelling place, and an eternal spiritual restoration. Thus all the elements of a national entity would be present. After Israel had broken her end of the Mosaic Covenant, she would be judged by God, through exile from her land, and Deut. 30, often referred to as the 'Land' or 'Palestinian' Covenant, provides more detailed promises which would fulfill aspects of the Abrahamic Covenant.

II Samuel 7 unveils further promise. Not only would Israel have an eternal dwelling, but she would have an eternal King, through the seed of David.

Jeremiah 31 records the introducing of the New Covenant with Israel. This is a replacement of the non-eternal, conditional Old Covenant, the Mosaic Law. This covenant promises eternal spiritual restoration, and forgiveness of sin, specifically for national Israel, as Pentecost explains,

Israel, according to this covenant, must be restored to the land of Palestine, which they will possess as their own. This also entails the preservation of the nation. Israel must experience a national conversion, be regenerated, receive the forgiveness of sins and the implantation of a new heart. This takes place following the return of Messiah to the earth. Israel must experience the outpouring of the Holy Spirit so that He may produce righteousness in the individual and teach the individual so that there will be the fulness of knowledge. Israel must receive material blessings from the hand of the King into whose kingdom they have come. Palestine must be reclaimed, rebuilt, and made the glorious center of a new glorious earth in which dwelleth righteousness and peace. The Messiah who came and shed His blood as the foundation of this covenant must personally come back to this earth to effect the salvation, restoration, and blessing of the national Israel. All of these important areas of eschatological study are made necessary by this covenant.[39]

These Covenants unlock the promises made to Abraham. The general promises will be kept in detail. Note that there are many promises made to Israel, namely, land, leadership, law, and citizenry. Many physical blessings even in addition to these are promised, which Israel will assuredly receive.

God's promises to the church are vastly different.

Israel was promised numerous physical and spiritual blessings, which Christ came (first advent) to consummate. Because of Israel's rejection of her King and Messiah (apex of that rejection recorded in Matt. 12, and John 12) Israel was set aside for a time, while the gentiles are grafted in to *one* of Israel's promises, that the Jews might be made jealous and return to her King. Romans 9-11 make this concept abundantly clear.

The gentiles would not be able to claim all of the promises made to Israel, for they were made to Abraham's physical seed, but recall in Genesis 12:3, that there was a blessing for all those who were not the seed of Abraham, through those who were. It becomes evident, as I John 2:25 explains, that this blessing is the ultimate promise to the church - eternal life.

The New Covenant of Jer. 31 promised a forgiveness of sins to Israel, and when Christ instituted the Lord's Supper, it became evident that the aspect of forgiveness of sins even touched the gentiles.

Israel seeks physical and spiritual restoration in an eternal, earthly kingdom, through many promises. The church has eternal life also, and seeks a heavenly kingdom through the singular promise of eternal life as revealed in all its details.

Thus because the two groups, in time, have different purposes in the grand design, the impetus which will drive the two groups toward their declared goals are unique and different. The church awaits that time when the focus will return to Israel, and the church will be removed from this earth. Israel awaits, unknowingly, the time of her judgment and refining - Jacob's trouble. The final heptad of Daniel's 70 (Dan. 9).

Therefore, to rightly understand God's plan in history, it is imperative to correctly ascertain the distinct purposes for Israel and the church. The impact of these purposes on Biblical theology is inarguably clear. Beginning with the bases of the various covenants, the purposes for the two groups, Israel and the church, in a system of literal interpretation, become vastly unique, only occasionally touching one another (doing so especially in regard to salvation and the forgiveness of sins).   As a result, the approach one takes to his understanding of the roles of Israel and the church will direct his understanding of Scripture to the farthest reach of one side or the other.

CHAPTER VIII

PROMISES EXPOUNDED
THE NEW TESTAMENT

Background
The Inter-Testamental Period[40]

The Old Testament closes with Israel under the subjection of the Persian Empire, which maintained their dominance until the rise of Alexander the Great, who warred against the Persian Empire in 334 BC, gaining ultimate victory in just a few short years, and in doing so led Greece to swift world dominance. His empire crumbled as quickly as it had been built, as he became ill with fever and died in 323 BC.

His kingdom was divided among his four generals in fulfillment of Daniel's prophecy (Dan. 8:21-26): Cassander, ruled over Macedonia; Lysimachus, over Thrace and Asia Minor; Seleucus, over Syria and Babylonia; and Ptolemy, over Egypt and Arabia.

The Ptolemies exercised authority over Israel, but were tolerant and fairly uninvolved, as the Jews were allowed to continue their worship and culture. Under Ptolemy Philadelphus (285-247 BC) the Old Testament was translated at Alexandria into the Greek translation known as the Septuagint.

Wars between the Ptolemies and Seleucids alternated control over Palestine until Antiochus Epiphanes ascended to the Seleucid throne in 175 BC. Antiochus, the new Syrian king, took the city of Jerusalem and pillaged the temple, even sacrificing a pig in the temple[41].

This outrage resulted in revolts initially led by a Jewish priest named Mattathias, and later by his son Judas Maccabeus.

Maccabeus was victorious over Lysias, Antiochus' appointed governor, in 165 BC, which brought about the purification of the temple and the resumption of worship. The annual feast of Hanukkah celebrates this event.

The continued threat of Hellenization was influential in creating divisions among the Jews. The scribes and priests initially were united in message, but as the priests and rulers succumbed to the Greek influence their concern for the Torah diminished. The scribes, however, remained committed to the Torah. The distinctions grew so strong that by the time of Judas Maccabeus, two sects had evolved - the Pharisees from the scribes, and the Sadducees from the priests and rulers.

In order to ensure obedience to the written Law the Pharisees developed a massive body of oral laws, against which the Sadducees rebelled. The Pharisees, to their credit recognized a distinction between the spiritual, and thus acknowledged the resurrection, while the Sadducees were strictly temporal, focusing as a result strictly on the political independence of Israel, and on the Temple as the cultural center, (the Pharisees began to utilize synagogues). As a result, when the Temple was destroyed in 70 AD, the Sadducees ceased to exist. Two additional sects grew to prominence as well: the Essenes emphasized moral purity, and in contrast to the Sadducees, they believed in the immortality of the soul, also they made immersion baptism prominent; the Zealots were appropriately named, as they vigorously pursued political independence for Israel.

In 138 BC, Antiochus VII sought to regain influence over Palestine which had been lost by the revolts, but in 129 BC, Antiochus died in battle, ending the Seleucid dynasty.

Following Antiochus' death, John Hyrcanus of the Hasmonean (or Maccabean) family led Judea to a brief golden age until his death in 104 BC.

Although the Hasmonean dynasty continued, civil war characterized the next years until Pompey of Rome intervened by taking Jerusalem in 63 BC. The Maccabean family tried to thwart Roman rule for the next thirty years, but the Roman grip was strong.

Rome at that time was ruled by a triumvirate of Julius Caesar, Crassus, and Pompey. After the death of Crassus (53 BC) there was a brief civil war between Caesar and Pompey. Caesar emerged victorious, and after a brief dictatorship, Julius Caesar was killed (44 BC) and his kingdom was transferred to his grandnephew Octavian, who became Augustus Caesar.

Augustus Caesar, renowned for his reforms and emphasis on senatorial rule, presided over Rome as the first consolidated Roman emperor from 44 BC to 14 AD. Upon his death, his stepson Tiberius ascended to the throne. He became known as Tiberius Julius Caesar Augustus. Tiberius ruled actively until 26 AD, and it was during his reign that the Messiah appeared.

Appointed by Caesar as king of Judea, Herod the Great ruled until 4 BC, and it was during his rule in Judea that the Christ was born.

Inter-Testamental Jewish Teachings

Midrash – system of interpretation of the Tanak, in two sections: midrash halaka – handled legal texts; midrash haggada – handled historical texts

Mishnah – codified oral traditions of the Torah

Gemara – commentary on the Mishnah

Talmud – the combined Mishnah & Gemara

Midrashim – individual midrashic commentaries including Midrash Rabbah (on the Torah and Five Scrolls) and Pesikta Midrashim (on festivals)

Background

The New Testament contains twenty-seven books, inspired by God (II Tim. 3:16), written by nine authors over a period of roughly fifty years. The divisions of books are:

I. Six Historical Books: The Four Gospels:

1. **Matthew** 45 AD – presents Messiah as King

2. **Mark** 50-60 AD – presents Messiah as Servant

3. **Luke** 60 AD – presents Messiah as Man

4. **John** 60-69 AD – presents Messiah as God

5. The **Acts** of the Apostles 63 AD – recounts birth and early years of the church

6. **Revelation** 85-95 AD – a historical book in the sense that much of it was the history of the end times viewed in advance. This is *not* to say that the events have been historically fulfilled, rather that what is spoken of are literal events yet to be fulfilled – history in the making. The book characterizes itself as prophecy.

II. Thirteen Pauline Epistles:

1 & 2. I & II Thessalonians 50-51 AD – New Covenant growth & hope

3 & 4. **I & II Corinthians** 54-55 AD – New Covenant unity and ministry

5. **Galatians** 56 AD – New Covenant economy

6. **Romans** 57 AD – New Covenant righteousness

7. **Philippians** 61 AD – New Covenant walk despite affliction

8. **Philemon** 63 AD – New Covenant repentance & forgiveness

9. **Ephesians** 63 AD – New Covenant wealth

10. **Colossians** 63 AD – New Covenant walk in the all-sufficient Christ

11. **I Timothy** 65 AD – New Covenant godliness

12. **Titus** 65 AD – New Covenant purity

13. **II Timothy** 67-68 AD – New Covenant conduct

III. Eight General Epistles:

1. **James** 48 AD – addresses New Covenant conduct

2. **Hebrews** 64-67 AD – the majesty of the Son

3. & 4. **I & II Peter** 65-67 AD – New Covenant holiness & diligence

5. **Jude** 65-67 AD – a call to contend for the faith

6., 7., & 8. **I, II, & III John** 80-85 AD - New Covenant fellowship, truth, & hospitality

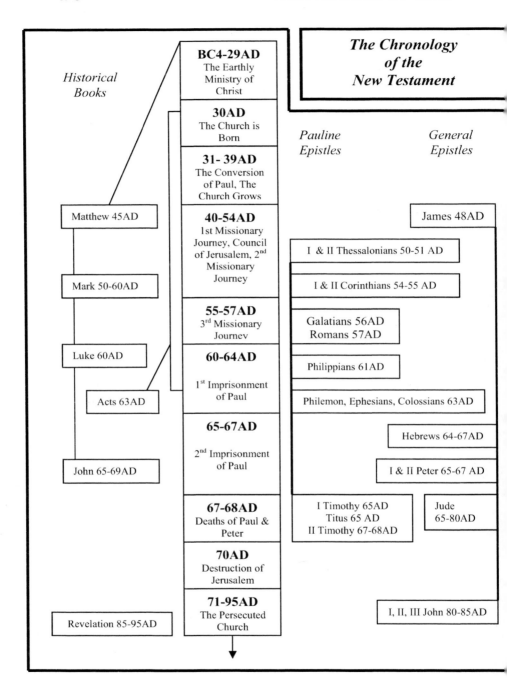

The Chronology of the New Testament

Historical Books

Pauline Epistles

General Epistles

BC4-29AD The Earthly Ministry of Christ		
30AD The Church is Born		
31- 39AD The Conversion of Paul, The Church Grows		
40-54AD 1st Missionary Journey, Council of Jerusalem, 2nd Missionary Journey		James 48AD
	I & II Thessalonians 50-51 AD	
	I & II Corinthians 54-55 AD	
55-57AD 3rd Missionary Journey	Galatians 56AD Romans 57AD	
60-64AD 1st Imprisonment of Paul	Philippians 61AD	
	Philemon, Ephesians, Colossians 63AD	
65-67AD 2nd Imprisonment of Paul		Hebrews 64-67AD
		I & II Peter 65-67 AD
67-68AD Deaths of Paul & Peter	I Timothy 65AD Titus 65 AD II Timothy 67-68AD	Jude 65-80AD
70AD Destruction of Jerusalem		
71-95AD The Persecuted Church		I, II, III John 80-85AD

Matthew 45AD

Mark 50-60AD

Luke 60AD

Acts 63AD

John 65-69AD

Revelation 85-95AD

CHAPTER IX

PROMISES EMBODIED
EARTHLY MINISTRY OF CHRIST

4 BC – AD 29

The Gospels: New Covenant Initiated

Matthew	Mark	Luke	John

Key Issues

The Messiah Presented ----Matt. 4:17;Mark 1:14-15;Luke 4:16-22;John 1:1-18

The Messiah Rejected --Matt. 12;Mark 3:22-30;Luke 11:14-36; John 10:22-39

The Church Prophesied ------------------------Matthew 16:13-20

The Timeline Expounded ----------Matt. 24; Mark 13; Luke 21

The New Covenant Initiated--Matt. 26:26-29; Mark 14:22-25;Luke 22:14-20

The 'Rapture' Promised ----------------------------------John 14:1-3

The Holy Spirit Promised ----------------John 14:16-31, 16:5-15

The New Covenant Ratified: The Sacrifice & Triumph of Messiah---------------------------- Matthew 27-28; Mark 15-16; Luke 23-24; John 18-21

Introduction to the Gospels

Distinct characteristics tie Matthew, Mark, and Luke together, while John's Gospel stands alone in its context. The first three gospels handle many of the events of Christ's life in detail, while the fourth focuses on seven specific signs, demonstrating the deity of Christ. The first three provide a more detailed narrative of the events of Jesus' earthly ministry, while John states plainly that his intention is to record only that information that would result in a saving belief in Christ:

> Many other signs therefore Jesus also performed in the presence of the disciples which are not written in this book; but these have been written that you may believe that Jesus is the Christ, the Son of God; and that believing you may have life in His name. (John 20:30-31).

It is commonly suggested in modern times that Mark wrote first because his writing was shorter than Matthew's or Luke's, because much of the information in the Gospel of Mark can be found in Mathew and Luke as well, and because of apparent grammatical refinements in Matthew and Luke. It appears that Mark wrote between 50-60 AD, and while it is possible that he was the earliest author, it is highly unlikely. Most who assume Mark's early authorship also assume that Matthew and Luke borrowed from him, due to the previous mentioned reasons.

Matthew was the only one of the first three Gospel writers to have been an eyewitness of Jesus. As one of the twelve Disciples of Christ he would have been very acquainted with the teachings and doings of the Savior. It seems most logical that his nearness to Christ would have allowed him to compose an 'original' Gospel – or at least from a human standpoint one who was with Jesus would not logically have to borrow information from one who was not.

It is most probable that Matthew did indeed write first and that his information came from his own eyewitness and the work of the Holy Spirit. This was also universally held in the very early church – and as a result has always been placed first in the New Testament.[42] Matthew could have written as early as 37-39 AD, but almost certainly no later than 45 AD, which would predate Mark's Gospel by at least several years.

Luke clearly did 'borrow' information, as he states this emphatically in the early going of his Gospel (1:1-3), probably from Matthew, Mark and possibly the testimony of other disciples as well. He makes no apology for his use of sources to compile his Gospel. Even so, the authority of his writings is certainly not compromised, as he bore the authority of a companion of Paul at the very least, was a missionary in his own right, and bears the unmistakable brand of truth upon his Gospel.

John wrote his Gospel at least before the destruction of Jerusalem in 70 AD, in part due to a present tense reference to Jerusalem (5:2).

The Documentary Hypothesis
The Q Theory

As mentioned earlier, it has become popular to assume that Matthew and Luke borrowed from Mark, but modern criticism extends farther and goes something like this:

According to the theory, Mark wrote the first Gospel, based upon the authority of Peter, and in parallel with the hypothetical source document referred to as 'Q'. Matthew then wrote, borrowing from unique sources, from Mark, and from Q. Finally, Luke wrote, but did not use Matthew's unique sources, in fact he didn't use Matthew at all, but rather used Mark and Q, as well as his own unique sources.

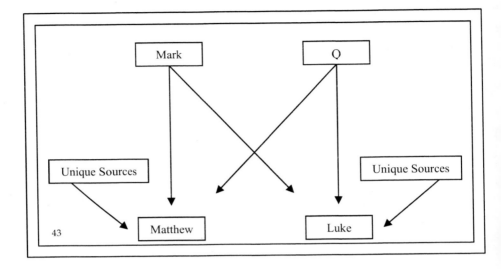

This theory seeks to explain difficult similarities and likenesses in the Gospel account, but it creates more problems than it solves. First, it assumes that God did not inspire the words of these individual men as independent, but rather used human sources to glean their information, and while Luke proclaims his use of sources (which very well could have been the other Gospels, as well as other oral traditions of the apostles which were not recorded in the Gospels); Matthew and Mark do not, which makes the documentary hypothesis a speculative leap. Second, it assumes that an eyewitness of Jesus (Matthew) borrowed from someone who was not with Jesus (Mark), creating a logical inconsistency with this hypothesis. And finally, it introduces 'other sources', including 'Q', for which there is no historical or Biblical evidence, again too speculative and assuming, and in result damaging the authority of the text.

The Gospel Genealogies

In order to meet the criteria to be Messiah, Christ had to come from the seed of David, he had to be of the tribe of Judah, in the line of Solomon (yet he could not be of the seed of Coniah, see Jer. 22:30) So it is with great care that Matthew and Luke demonstrate the lineage of Christ.

Matthew presents in his gospel the genealogy from Abraham to Joseph, the husband of Mary. Matthew itemizes fourteen generations from Abraham to David, fourteen from David to the Deportation, and fourteen from the Deportation to Christ. Not every name in the lineage of Christ is mentioned, as some were excluded (Ahaziah, Joash, Amaziah, Jehoiakim, & Eliakim, etc.) It is also significant that Matthew mentions women in his genealogy (highly unusual in Hebrew genealogies), specifically Tamar, Rahab, Ruth, Bathsheeba is alluded to but not named (possibly as a consequence for adultery), and of course Mary. (Also note that 42 generations are mentioned, yet only 41 names, as David is mentioned twice, giving the genealogy a poetic symmetry.[44]) Joseph, earthly father of Jesus, is identified as the son of Jacob.

Luke presents a different genealogy, tracing his to Adam. Again, there are gaps in the genealogies, as it was more important for the Hebrew genealogy to demonstrate legitimate descent rather than to present a complete listing. Luke provides a different listing than Matthew of David to Joseph, Luke's listing coming from Nathan the son of David rather than from Solomon (as Coniah was in the line of Solomon), and identifies Joseph as "of Eli", suggesting that Joseph was Eli's son in law, by virtue of his betrothal to Mary, and thus Luke actually presents the genealogy of Mary.

Matthew therefore traces Jesus' legal lineage and right to the throne through Joseph, enabling God to keep

His covenant promises made regarding Solomon, while
Luke traces Jesus' physical lineage through Mary, enabling
Him to avoid the curse of Coniah.

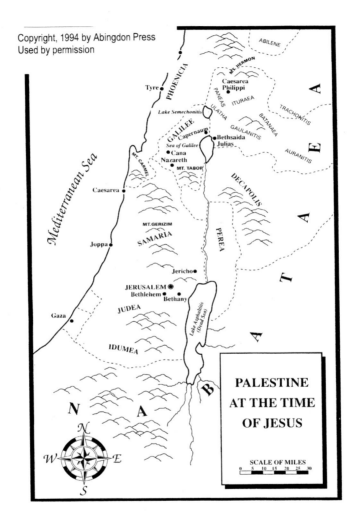

The Gospel of Matthew 45 AD

Matthew: The Servant King	His Ministry 4:18-26:46	His Preparation 1-4:11	1 His Genealogy & Birth
			2 His Authentication
			3 His Baptism
			4:1-11 His Perfection
		In Galilee & Judea	4:12-7:28 His Followers, Authority, & Message: Sermon on the Mount
			8-9 His Miracles: Leper, Centurion's Servant, Peter's Mother in Law
			10-11 His Messengers
			12 His Rejection
			13 His Parables
			14-15 His Compassion: Healings & Miracles
			16 His Program: The Church, His Death, & Discipleship
			17 His Glorification: Transfiguration & Authentication
			18-20:16 His Kingdom Conditions
			20:17-34 His Sacrifice Prophesied Again
		In Jerusalem	21:1-17 His Acknowledgment: Triumphal Entry & Temple Cleansing
			21:18-27 His Authority
			21:28-22:14 His Parables: 2 Sons, Landowner, & Marriage Feast
			22:15-46 His Testing: Regarding Caesar, Resurrection, Law, & Identity
			23 His Opponents: Scribes & Pharisees
			24-25 His Return: Olivet Discourse
			26:1-46 His Preparation For Death: New Covenant Ratified
		His Sacrifice & Triumph 26:47-28:20	26:47-27:26 His Betrayal & Trial
			27:27-66 His Crucifixion & Burial
			28 His Resurrection & Final Instruction

Key Issues

Background

Matthew is first identified in 9:9, and is referred to as a tax gatherer (10:3), and was also known as Levi, the son of Alphaeus (Mark 2:14). He was one of the twelve original disciples of Christ, and he is the author of the earliest gospel account, most probably written originally in Hebrew in 45 AD.

Christian tradition tells of Matthew's ministry to Ethiopia and Egypt, to whom he gave the gospel and even his life in martyrdom.[45]

Summary

Matthew focuses on the Messiah's identity as the Davidic King of Israel. He traces Messiah's genealogy through David, and records His birth, baptism, and testing in preparation for His Kingdom message.

Matthew 4:17
The Messiah Presented

The message the Messiah presented initially was

> Repent, for the kingdom of heaven is at hand.
> (4:17)

He offered the Davidic Kingdom to Israel at that time. Christ presented the Kingdom gospel (highlighted by His sermon on the Mount in 5-7) until that message was ultimately rejected in chapter 12.

Matthew 12
The Messiah Rejected

The response was a rejection of Jesus as Messiah and an accusation that His power came from Satan (12:24). This marked the unpardonable sin (12:30-32), and made their rejection of Him complete.

After this rejection, He spoke publicly in parables from that point on, so that the prophecy of Isaiah 6:9-10 would be fulfilled (13:14-15).

Matthew 16:13-20
The Church Prophesied

To His disciples, however, He spoke clearly, prophesying the coming of the church in Matthew 16:13-20.

The prophecy included the following elements:

1. The church would be built upon Christ.

Note that Christ referred to Simon as 'Peter', which is the Greek *petros*, and refers to a small stone. He then says "upon this rock (the Greek *petra*, referring to a boulder or a cliff – the same word is used in 7:24) I will build My church." (16:18). Peter understood clearly that the church would be built upon Christ, as he recognizes that truth in prophetic context in I Peter 2:6-10.

2. The church would not be defeated

Because of the strength of its Foundation, the church would stand against all opposition.

3. Peter would possess the 'keys to the kingdom'.

Peter fulfilled this role, being present as each people group first received the Holy Spirit (Jews in Acts 2, Samaritans in Acts 8:14-17, and the gentiles in Acts 10:44-45)

4. The apostles would have the authority of heaven.

Although specifically directed to Peter here, Christ reiterates later that the eleven would have unique authority (John 20:23). This would certainly include the authority to record the inspired word of God.

As the day of His death drew near, He gave his disciples a glimpse of things to come in the Olivet Discourse of chapters 24-25

Matthew 24
The Timeline Expounded

As the disciples were admiring the temple buildings, Christ cryptically tells them that they will be destroyed. They respond by asking Him two questions. (1) When will these things be? And (2) what will be the sign of Your coming and of the end of the age?

Christ answers the first question in 24:4-14, describing wars, famines, earthquakes, persecutions, false prophets, and lawlessness. But the gospel would be preached in the entire world as a witness. That would be a sign that the end was coming.

Christ answers the second question in 24:15-31, as He describes in vv.15-28 the last half of the seventieth week of Daniel (Daniel 9), referring to this time period as the "great tribulation" (v.21). The seven-year tribulation would encompass Jacob's Trouble (Jer. 30:7), but the second half of this period would be unimaginably severe, and would commence with the breaking of antichrist's covenant in the middle of the seven-year period (Matt. 24:15, Dan. 9:27).

Immediately after the tribulation the sign of His coming would appear (24:29-31), as the heavens would be shaken, and His elect would be assembled from heaven and the King would return (Rev. 19:11-14).

Matthew 26:26-29
The New Covenant Initiated

Just as the Abrahamic and Davidic Covenants were empty without the promise of forgiveness that the New Covenant brought, even so the coming of the King as described in ch. 24 would not have provided hope without the New Covenant, and so it is, that in the Upper Room Christ seals the New Covenant with His own blood which was to be poured out for the forgiveness of sin only a few short hours from that moment.

Matthew 27-28
The New Covenant Ratified
The Sacrifice & Triumph of Messiah

The Messiah King was crucified, just as prophesied. He was buried and rose again, just as He said. Israel had rejected her King, but God's purpose would soon become apparent, as He would provide New Covenant forgiveness not just for Israel, but for all nations and peoples, thus fulfilling the Abrahamic promise of blessing to all the families of the earth (Gen. 12:3).

The Gospel of Mark   50-60 AD

Mark: The Sovereign Servant		In Preparation 1:1-13		1:1-8	The Forerunner
				1:9-11	The Baptism
				1:12-13	The Testing
	In Galilee 1:14-9:50		Message	1:14-15	Message Proclaimed
				1:16-20	Personnel of the Message
				1:21-2:12	Authority of the Message
				2:13-3:6	Nature of the Message
				3:7-5:21	Preaching of the Message
				5:22-43	Substance of the Message: Faith
				6:1-6	Origination of the Message
				6:7-30	Preaching of the Message
			Servant	6:31-44	His Compassion
				6:45-56	His Power
				7:1-23	His Attitude Toward Tradition
				7:24-8:9	His Compassion
			Response	8:10-9:10	Blindness
				9:11-50	Misunderstanding
	10 In Perea			10	Hardness of Heart
	In Jerusalem 11:1-16:20		Servant	11:1-33	As a King
				12:1-34	His Rejection
				12:35-44	His Acceptance
				13	As a Prophet
				14:1-9	His Anointing
				14:10-11	His Betrayer
				14:12-25	His New Covenant
				14:26-42	His Preparation
			Service	14:43-52	His Betrayal
				14:53-65	Before the High Priest
				14:66-72	His Disciple's Denial
				15:1-14	Before Pilate
				15:15-41	His Crucifixion
				15:42-47	His Burial
				16:1-8	His Resurrection
				16:9-18	Before Witnesses
				16:19-20	His Ascension

Key Issues

Background

John Mark is identified as Peter's son in the faith (I Pet. 5:13), and there is consensus among early church writers that Mark served as Peter's interpreter while Peter was in Rome.[46] Eusebius tells the tradition of how Mark's gospel came into being:

> So brightly shone the light of true religion on the minds of Peter's hearers [in Rome] that, not satisfied with a single hearing or with the oral teaching of the divine message, they resorted to appeals of every kind to induce Mark (whose gospel we have), as he was a follower of Peter, to leave them in writing a summary of the instruction they had received by word of mouth, nor did they let him go till they had persuaded him, and thus became responsible for the writing of what is known as the Gospel according to Mark.[47]

Later quoting Papias, Eusebius explains that Mark's purpose was to record everything he had heard from Peter (although not necessarily in order), and to be totally accurate in what he wrote.[48]

Origen, the early church father, asserted that Mark wrote his gospel at the instruction of Peter.[49]

Mark's gospel has generally been recognized as having the authority of Peter (in addition to Mark's own authority as a faithful servant of Christ), and the inspiration of the Holy Spirit. Date of authorship is between 50 and 60 AD.

Mark is initially identified as John Mark (Acts 12:12). He accompanied Barnabas and Paul on the First missionary Journey (Acts 12:25; 13:5), but left before the journey was complete (13:13), causing division between Barnabas and Paul regarding his involvement in the Second Missionary Journey (15:37). John Mark was soon restored in Paul's estimation, as he would later call John Mark a "fellow worker" and a "comfort to me" (Philemon 24; Col. 4:10-11), and he expressed a desire for John Mark to join him for he was "helpful to me in my ministry" (2 Tim 4:11).

Mark also ministered in Egypt, being influential in the conversions of many in Alexandria, and serving as the first bishop there before being martyred under the Roman Emperor, Nero.[50]

Summary

Mark presents the Messiah as the Son of God, and the servant of God. It is a gospel of action, utilizing the term 'immediately' forty-two times, and demonstrating Christ's focus and purpose in accomplishing His sacrificial service.

Mark 1:14-15
The Messiah Presented

The ministry of Messiah begins with His presentation of the arrival of the Davidic Promise:

> The time is fulfilled, and the kingdom of God is at hand; repent and believe in the gospel. (1:14-15)

The Kingdom was clearly offered to Israel.

Mark 3:22-30
The Messiah Rejected

As is recorded in Matthew, the Kingdom offer was rejected, as His own people (3:21) attributed His power to Satan. This was blasphemy of the work of the Holy Spirit, the unpardonable sin (3:29). The Messiah's ministry then became one of judgment, speaking in parables in order that the rejecting generation might not repent.

Mark 13
The Timeline Expounded

As in Matthew 24, the disciples ask Jesus two questions: (1) when will the destruction of the temple buildings be, and (2) what will be the sign of the fulfillment of all things. Jesus responds to the first question in vv. 6-13, describing wars, earthquakes, famines, and persecutions; and to the second in vv. 14-27, as He describes the latter half of the tribulation period, which would immediately precede the sign and commencement of His 2nd Coming.
The application to the disciples was: Be alert! (13:37)

Mark 14:22-25
The New Covenant Initiated

As Jesus prepares for His sacrificial service, He initiates the New Covenant at the Last Supper. It is His blood, and no one else's, upon which the New Covenant promises stood. Like the Abrahamic Covenant, it was initiated only by God and therefore, the promises were unconditional, and they were assured.

Mark 15-16
The New Covenant Ratified
The Sacrifice & Triumph of Messiah

The suffering Servant of Isaiah 53 had fulfilled prophecy, and had completed His sacrifice. His next coming would not be as a humble and suffering servant, but rather as the Messiah King, who would install the promised Kingdom.

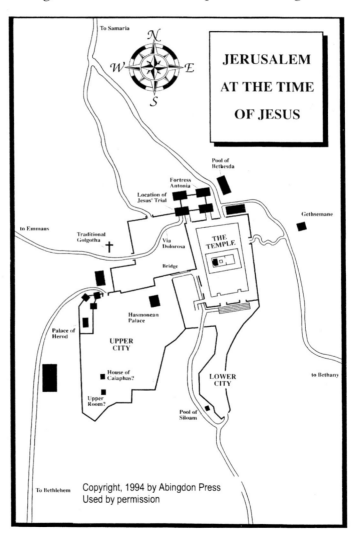

The Gospel of Luke   60 AD

Luke: The Sovereign Son Of Man	**His Ministry**	**His Preparation** 1-4:13	1-2:20 Prophecies & Births of John & Jesus
			2:21-4:13 His Preparation: Youth, Baptism, & Testing
			4:14-30 His Presentation: Teaching In The Synagogue
		In Galilee & Judea (4:14-21:46)	4:31-6:19 His Authority (Miracles) & Followers (Disciples)
			6:20-49 His Teachings
			7-8:3 His Compassion: Centurion's Servant, John, The Sinful Woman
			8:4-9:27 His Authority (Miracles) & Followers (Disciples)
			9:28-36 His Glorification: Transfiguration
			9:37-62 His Program: Death, Purpose of His Coming, & Discipleship Cost
			10:1-24 His Messengers: The 70
			10:25-11:13 His Teaching: The Good Samaritan, Priority, & Prayer
			11:14-54 His Rejection
			12 His Warnings: On Hypocrisy, Greed, Anxiety, Readiness, Stewardship
			13 His Willingness To Forgive
			14-16 His Parables: Wedding Feast, Dinner, Cost Of Discipleship, Lost Sheep, Lost Coin, Prodigal Son, Unrighteous Steward, Rich Man & Lazarus
			17-18:8 His Instructions To Disciples: Faith, Gratitude, 2nd Coming, Prayer
			18:9-34 His Instructions: Humility, Faith, Commitment, Death & Resurrection
			18:35-19:10 His Followers: Bartamaeus & Zaccheus
		In Jerusalem	19:11-48 His Kingdom Misunderstood: Parable of the Minas, Triumphal Entry, Cleansing of the Temple
			20:1-18 His Authority
			20:19-44 His Testing: Regarding Caesar, Resurrection
			20:45-21:4 His Teaching: On Acceptable Worship
			21:5-38 His Prophetic Plan
			22:1-46 His Preparation For Death: New Covenant Ratified
	His Sacrifice & Triumph 22:47-24:53		22:47-23:25 His Betrayal, Arrest, & Trial
			23:26-56 His Crucifixion & Burial
			24 His Resurrection, Appearances, & Ascension

Key Issues

Background

Luke is identified by Paul as 'the beloved physician' (Col. 4:14), and a fellow worker of Paul (Philemon 24), and as a gentile (Col 4:11). Eusebius maintains that he was from Antioch[51] (a possible explanation for the emphasis of Antioch in the book of Acts). He remained a faithful friend of Paul, and was the last one standing with him as Paul wrote his final epistle (II Tim. 4:11). His authorship of the Gospel of Luke, with Acts as its sequel, is unquestionable, as all the Greek manuscripts ascribe it to him.[52] The date of authorship was most likely 60 AD. He gained his authority from those who were eyewitnesses (Luke 1:2).

The location and scope of Luke's activity after the martyrdom of Paul is not recorded. The nature of his death is also surrounded by the same uncertainty. Some suggest he was martyred, but there is no historical evidence either way.[53]

Luke identifies his Gospel, the longest of the four, as a compilation of events according to eyewitnesses (1:1-2). He addresses the Gospel to Theophilus (possibly an official at Antioch), and assures him it is the exact truth (1:4). He refers to this gospel in his introduction to the book of Acts (1:1).

Summary

Luke presents Jesus as the Son of Man, emphasizing the human birth of Messiah (2:11), His perfection as a Man (4:13), and His mission as the One qualified to save (19:10).

His Gospel is characterized by compassion for the poor and the oppressed, and his emphasizing of these themes as Christ made evident demonstrates something of Luke's own compassionate disposition.

Luke 4:16-22
The Messiah Presented

The presentation of Messiah in Luke points to a different event than does Matthew or Mark. Here Jesus is seen entering the synagogue, reading from Isaiah 61:1-2, a passage regarding Messiah's role as an anointed Man who would bring a message of deliverance to the oppressed. Jesus ascribes Himself as the fulfillment of the passage. The immediate response was one of rejection.

Luke 11:14-36
The Messiah Rejected

There were numerous other opportunities for the Jews to accept Him, and the ultimate rejection came as the people attributed His power to Satan (v. 15), as recorded in Matthew and Mark.

Luke 21
The Timeline Expounded

As in Matthew and Mark, Luke records the disciples questions, and Jesus' response as He describes false christs, wars and disturbances, earthquakes, plagues and famines, signs in the heavens and persecutions (21:8-19), followed by the tribulation period which would culminate in His 2nd Coming (21:20-28)

Luke 22:14-20
The New Covenant Initiated

Like Matthew and Mark, Luke recounts the cup at the Last Supper, symbolic of His blood poured out to seal the New Covenant. As the perfect Man, only He was qualified to serve in the substitutionary role that Messiahship would require (Isaiah 53).

Luke 23-24
The New Covenant Ratified
The Sacrifiec & Triumph of Messiah

Includes His trial, death, burial, resurrection, and appearances, which again emphasized His perfection and qualification as Messiah. The prophecies spoke of Him:

> 'These are My words which I spoke to you while I was still with you, that all things which are written about Me in the Law of Moses and the Prophets and the Psalms must be fulfilled.' Then He opened their minds to understand the Scriptures. (24:44-45)

The Gospel of John   65-69 AD

The Gospel of John: The God-Man: That You May Believe	Presentation	1-12	1:1-34	The Word & His Witness
			1:35-51	His Disciples
			2:1-12	His 1st Sign: Water Into Wine
			2:13-25	His Zeal: Cleansing the Temple
			3:1-21	His Teaching: 2nd Birth: Nicodemus
			3:22-36	His Witness: John's Teaching
			4:1-45	His Compassion: The Woman at the Well
			4:46-54	His 2nd Sign: Healing the Royal Official's Son
			5	His 3rd Sign (Healing on the Sabbath) & Explanation (4 Witnesses)
			6	His 4th & 5th Signs (Feeding 5k, Walk on Water) & Explanation (Bread of Life)
			7:1-52	His Authority: Teaching at the Feast of Booths
			7:53-8:11	His Mercy: Woman Caught in Adultery
			8:12-8:59	His Presentation & Rejection
			9-10	His 6th Sign (Healing the Man Born Blind) & Explanation (His Deity)
			11:1-46	His 7th Sign (Lazarus Raised) & Explanation (Resurrection & Life)
			11:47-57	His Opponents: Chief Priests & Pharisees
			12	His Hour Begun: Anointing by Mary, Triumphal Entry, Death Foretold
	Explanation	13-17	13-14	His Disciples Prepared: His Example, Betrayal Foretold, Spirit Promised
			15	His Instruction: Parable of the Vine, Command to Love, Hatred by the World
			16	His Warnings: Hatred by the World, Holy Spirit Promised, His Program
			17	His Prayer
	Verification	18-21	18	His Betrayal, Arrest, & Trial
			19	His Crucifixion & Burial
			20-21	His Resurrection & Appearances

Key Promises

The Messiah Presented ------------------------------John 1:1-18
The Messiah Rejected ----------------------------John 10:22-39
The Rapture Promised ----------------------------John 14:1-3
The Holy Spirit Promised --------------John 14:16-31, 16:5-15
The New Covenant Ratified ------------------------John 18-21

Background

John is identified as the brother of James, the son of Zebedee (Mark 1:19). He was a fisherman, with his brother, and partner of Simon (Mark 1:20; Luke 5:10). It appears that he was first a disciple of John the Baptist and soon came to know Jesus (1:35-39), ultimately receiving the call to apostleship (Mark 1:20).

He refers to himself in his Gospel as 'the disciple whom Jesus loved' (13:23; 19:26). Not only did he occupy a special place in Jesus' heart, he also would have a very unique ministry (21:18-24), for in addition to writing his Gospel of John (in 65-69 AD), and the I, II, & III Epistles of John, he also authored the Revelation of Jesus Christ, viewing first hand the future events that would ultimately fulfill the promises of God.

After the ascension of Christ, John ministered with the apostles in Jerusalem (Acts 3:1; 4:3-21; 8:1) and was later exiled to the island of Patmos, probably by Domitian (90-95 AD) for the preaching of the Gospel (Rev. 1:9). It was there that he completed his Apocalypse.

Summary

John's Gospel is distinct from the three Synoptic Gospels, for rather than presenting a thorough narrative of the miracles and activities of Christ, as the Synoptics did, John presents only seven signs.

His purpose for listing only these seven is stated in 20:30-31:

> Many other signs therefore Jesus also performed in the presence of the disciples, which are not written in this book; but these have been written that you may believe that Jesus is the Christ, the Son of God; and that believing you may have life in His name.

John writes his Gospel as an apologetic for the deity of Christ, demonstrating that He was the Messiah, the Son of God, and that He was One with God, and that He was God (1:1). The seven signs pointed to His inarguable identity.

The 7 Signs

1. Water into wine ----------------------2:1-12
2. Healing the official's son -----------4:46-54
3. Healing on the Sabbath --------------------5
4. Feeding of five thousand ------------6:1-14
5. Walking on water --------------------6:15-25
6. Healing the man born blind ----------------9
7. Raising of Lazarus ------------------11:1-44

In addition to the seven signs, John utilized contrasts to further bolster his conclusion: light vs. darkness (1:4–9), love vs. hatred (15:17, 18), from above vs. from below (8:23), life vs. death (6:57, 58), and truth vs. falsehood (8:32–47).

John 1:1-18
The Messiah Presented

John presents the Messiah clearly as God (1:1), as the Word, Who is the very essence of the revelation of God (1:18). He presents Messiah as Creator and Originator of life (1:3,4). And he presents Messiah's rejection as unnatural, for light illumines darkness.

John 10:22-39
The Messiah Rejected

As in the other Gospels, the rejection by the nation came in the form of an attributing of Jesus' power to the demonic (10:20), this in response to His 6th sign. Mercifully, He performs yet another sign (the raising of Lazarus, ch. 11), but the response is more severe: a plot to put Him to death.

John 14:1-3
Rapture Promised

Although not termed as such here, when coupled with Paul's revelation of the rapture (from the Latin term *rapto*, for *caught up*) in I Thessalonians 4:13-18, and I Corinthians 15:50-58, it is clearly the same event.
Jesus says,

> And if I go to prepare a place for you, I will come again, and receive you to Myself; that where I am, there you may be also.

This event alludes to the Jewish wedding tradition, in which the groom would leave his betrothed and prepare a place for her. At the completion of this time the groom would journey to meet his betrothed. They would meet each other half way, and he would bring her to his home.

By the language of this text, the 2nd Coming of Christ is not in view, as when He returns to the earth, He returns with His bride (Rev. 19:11-14).

John 14:16-31; 16:5-15
The Holy Spirit Promised

Christ promises, in these passages, the coming of the Holy Spirit (in fulfillment of Joel 2:28), for the purpose of giving the disciples remembrance of the truth, that they might write inspired words of God (14:26; 16:13-14; II Tim. 3:16), as well as convicting the world of sin, righteousness, and judgment (16:8), fulfilling His ministry according to prophecy. He would also disclose things to come (16:13), as He disclosed to John in the final Book of the Bible.

John 18-21
The New Covenant Ratified
The Sacrifice & Triumph of Messiah

Only God could forgive sin. Only God was perfect. Only God had the power over death. John demonstrates these characteristics of Jesus. He indeed was the Messiah. He is the Promised One through Whom God would keep His promises.

CHAPTER X

PROMISES UNVEILED
THE BRIDE OF CHRIST

AD 29 - ???

Historical Book

The Acts of the Apostles
AD 29-63

Pauline Epistles

Eschatology   *Soteriology*   *Christology*

I Thessalonians | II Thessalonians | I Corinthians | II Corinthians | Galatians | Romans | Philippians | Philemon | Ephesians | Colossians

Ecclesiology

I Timothy | Titus | II Timothy

General Epistles

James | Hebrews | I Peter | II Peter | Jude | I John | II John | III John

Key Issues

The Church Is Born --Acts 2

The Mystery of the Church: Salvation to the Gentiles ---Acts 10-11:18; Eph. 3:1-6; 5:28-32

The Hope Of The Church: The Rapture------------------I Thess. 4:13-18; I Cor. 15:50-58

The Economy Of The Church ---Galatians 3-4

The Timeline Gap --Romans 9-11

The Scope Of The Church --Ephesians 1:3

The Promise: Eternal Life ---I John 2:25

The Acts of the Apostles   63 AD

The Acts of the Apostles: The New Covenant Church				
	Jerusalem	Ministry of Peter	1	Commission & Preparation of the Disciples
			2	Pentecost: Coming of the Holy Spirit, Peter's Explanation, Church Born
			3	Peter's Miracle (Lame Beggar Healed) & Explanation
			4:1-31	Peter & John Arrested & Released
			4:32-5:11	Purifying the Church: Ananias & Saphira
			5:12-42	Peter & Apostles Arrested & Released
			6:1-7	Leadership In the Church: Seven Men Chosen
	Judea/Samaria		6:8-8:3	Stephen's Ministry, Arrest, Defense, & Murder
			8:4-25	Philip, Peter, & John in Samaria
			8:26-40	Philip & the Ethiopian Eunuch
			9:1-31	Saul's Conversion & Early Ministry
			9:32-43	Peter In Joppa: Raising of Tabitha
	Outermost Parts of the Earth		10-11:18	Salvation & The Holy Spirit to the Gentiles: Peter & Cornelius
			11:19-30	The Church at Antioch: First Called Christians
			12:1-23	Arrest & Release of Peter & Death of Herod
		Ministry of Paul	12:24-14:28	1st Missionary Journey: Paul, Barnabus, & John Mark
			15:1-35	Council of Jerusalem & James' Leadership
			15:36-18:22	2nd Missionary Journey: Paul & Silas
			18:23-21:26	3rd Missionary Journey
			21:27-40	Paul Arrested
			22-23:11	Paul's Defense Before the Jews & the Sanhedrin
			23:12-35	Paul Protected: Paul's Nephew Uncovers Assassination Plot
			24	Paul's Defense before Felix
			25:1-12	Paul's Defense Before Festus: Appeal to Caesar
			25:13-26:32	Paul's Defense Before Agrippa
			27-28	Paul Journeys To Rome

Key Issue

The Church is Born --Acts 2
The Mystery of the Church:
Salvation to the Gentiles -------------------------Acts 10-11:18

Authorship

See background on Luke

Background

The book of Acts is the sequel to Luke's Gospel, as Luke ties the book to his previous compilation (1:1), and it continues where Luke's Gospel left off. It forms the historical backbone of the New Testament as the church began. The events concluding the book (28:30) take place in about 63 AD, yet the final events of Paul's life (64 AD) are not here recorded. The most appropriate date, then, for authorship is 63 AD.

The transitional nature of the book must be noted, as history moves from one dispensation to the next. The history recorded in Acts covers that transition, and the scope of the book is historical, recording the events of transition, and is not intended as a theological primer. That function is served by the Epistles which would soon appear.

Summary

The outline for early church history is found in Jesus' instructions to the disciples before His ascension:

> And you shall be My witnesses both in Jerusalem, and in all Judea and Samaria, and even to the remotest part of the earth. (1:8b)

The book can be further divided by the ministries of its two most prominent apostles, Peter and Paul.

Acts 2
The Church is Born

After the ascension of Christ, the day of Pentecost found the disciples all in one place in Jerusalem, as the Holy Spirit descended upon them, and they began to speak in tongues. The text here is very clear on the meaning, as many who were making pilgrimage to Jerusalem heard the gospel in their native tongues (2:6-13). As Peter explained (2:15-36), this was to fulfill the prophecy of Joel 2:28, that God's Spirit would be poured out in the last days. This also fulfilled Jesus' promise that the Helper would come (John 14,16). In this context, speaking in tongues was literally the ability for the Jewish disciples, by the power of the Holy Spirit, to preach the gospel in languages they had never learned, for the purpose of authenticating that the end times ministry of the Holy Spirit had begun, and thus initiated the last days. This was the 'times of the gentiles' spoken of by Jesus (Luke 21:23-24), the gap in Daniel's seventieth week (Dan. 9), and the church age that Jesus promised (Matt. 16:13-20). The church was born.

Acts 3-8:3
The Church in Jerusalem

The gospel message spread quickly, via the preaching ministries of the apostles, but just as Christ was persecuted, His messengers were also. The church, possibly after growing too comfortable in Jerusalem, was forced outward by severe persecutions, including arrests of apostles, and ultimately the murder of Stephen, which was approved by a zealous Pharisee named Saul (8:1).

Acts 8:4-11:18
The Church in Judea & Samaria

The church expanded north into Samaria, led by the preaching of Philip. When it was evident that the gospel was being received in Samaria, Peter and John made their way there, and the Samaritans received the Holy Spirit (8:15).

In the meantime, Saul, the persecutor of the church, meets Jesus on the road to further persecutions at Damascus (9:1-9). He would be a chosen instrument, called as an apostle, to minister primarily to the gentiles, and before kings, and the sons of Israel (9:15).

But God was not yet finished with Peter. Recall Jesus' entrusting Peter with the keys to the kingdom (Matt. 16:19). Peter would be present as the ministry of the Holy Spirit was offered to each people group. Already, he had been present as both the Jews and Samaritans received the Holy Spirit, but next came something unimaginable, even for Peter.

Acts 10-11:18
Salvation to the Gentiles

The Abrahamic Covenant had promised blessing on the families of the earth (Gen. 12:3). The New Covenant promised forgiveness of sin for the Jews (Jer. 31). Joel 2:28 had promised the pouring out of the Holy Spirit upon gentiles as well.

God used Peter to bring the gospel to a gentile named Cornelius, who believed, he and those with him, they received forgiveness of sins (10:43), the Holy Spirit (10:44). God had given the New Covenant promise of forgiveness (and therefore eternal life) and the Holy Spirit to the gentiles. The Jewish believers were amazed (10:45).

Acts 11:19-12:23
The Church in the Outermost Parts, part 1

Peter's ministry would continue, and the church expansion would continue into the region of Antioch, where believers were given the name Christians as a term of derision (11:26). The persecution would continue with the murder of James, the brother of John and the arrest of Peter, but God would use another apostle to further preach the gospel message to the gentiles and to continue the growth of the young church.

*During this time **Matthew** completed his Gospel (45 AD).

Ministry of Paul

Acts 12:24-28:31
The Church in the Outermost Parts part 2

Paul was born in Tarsus (Acts 22:3), and was a Pharisee, of the tribe of Benjamin (Phil. 3:5). He also had the privilege of Roman citizenship (Acts 22:25-28). He was by trade, a tent maker (Acts 18:3), while his study of the Law came under Gamaliel (Acts 22:3). He was known by two names, Saul and Paul (Acts 13:9).

> The usual theory is that the apostle had a Jewish name, Saul, and a Roman name, Paul...But it is best to understand that Saul's name was changed as a matter of course when he became a Christian, that the word Paul means 'little', and that Paul wanted to be known as the 'little one' in Christ's service.[54]

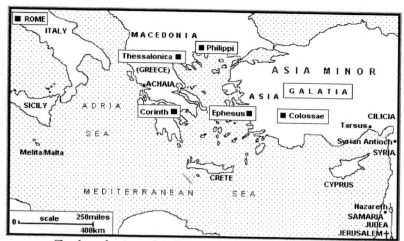

    Zealously involved in persecuting the church (Acts 8:1), Paul met Christ on the road to Damascus, and was called to be an apostle (Acts 9).

    The church continued to grow as Paul embarked on three Missionary Journeys to various parts of Asia Minor, proclaiming the gospel of salvation to the gentiles. The First was with Barnabas and John Mark (who did not finish the journey).

    Shortly after the completion of the First Missionary Journey of Paul, the natural growing pains of a united body of Jews and gentiles became evident. Through controversy regarding the application of Mosaic Law (or lack thereof) to Christians, a Council was held in Jerusalem (15), which was presided over by James the half-brother of Jesus, who acknowledged the Christian unity of the two groups, and encouraged the Jews in their freedom from the Law, and encouraged the gentiles in sensitivity toward the Jewish heritage.

*During this time **James** completed his Epistle (48 AD).

Paul's Second Missionary Journey took place shortly after the Council of Jerusalem, and after some disagreement with Barnabas regarding the inclusion of John Mark (15:38-39) the two split company, Paul choosing Silas, and Barnabas choosing John Mark (whose history in this regard is recounted in my introduction to the Gospel of Mark).

* During this time Paul wrote **I & II Thessalonians** (50-51 AD).
Paul's Third Missionary journey was something of a farewell tour, and it included a two-year ministry in Ephesus (19:8,10)

* During this time Paul wrote **I & II Corinthians** (54-55 AD).
* During this time **Mark** wrote his Gospel (50-60 AD)

His intention was to return to Jerusalem (bringing a contribution from Macedonia and Achaia to the poorer believers in Jerusalem, Rom. 15:26) and ultimately to visit Rome (19:21).

* During this time, Paul wrote **Galatians** (56 AD, although some suggest plausibly an earlier date, just after the Council of Jerusalem) and **Romans** (57 AD).

He did return to Jerusalem where he was arrested and sent to Rome where he would be twice imprisoned. The first of which was roughly from 60-64 AD, the beginning of which is documented in the conclusion of Acts (28:11-31).

* During this time **Luke** wrote his Gospel (60 AD), and Paul wrote his four prison Epistles: **Philippians** (61 AD), **Philemon** (63 AD), **Colossians** (63 AD), and **Ephesians** (63 AD).
* During the latter part of Paul's first imprisonment in Rome, Luke completed the book of **Acts** (63 AD)
Paul regained his freedom for a short time between 64-65 AD (implied by I Tim. 1:3), evidently spending the winter in Nicopolis (Titus 3:12). Nero had burned Rome, blaming the Christians, and it is speculated that Nero released Paul to ease tensions and minimize criticism of himself.[55]

* During this time Paul wrote **I Timothy** (65 AD), encouraging him to stay on at Ephesus, and shortly thereafter wrote to **Titus** (66-67 AD), encouraging him to remain strong in Crete (Titus 1:5).

Nero continued his persecution of the Christians, and after enjoying a brief period of freedom, Paul was again imprisoned in Rome.

* During this time Apollos (in the opinion of this writer) wrote **Hebrews** (64-67), and Peter wrote **I & II Peter** (65-67 AD), to encourage Christians amidst this severe persecution. The half brother of Jesus, **Jude** (65-67 AD) also wrote with the same theme in mind. The Gospel of **John** (65-69 AD) was also completed during this time. Paul also completed his last letter, **II Timothy** (67-68 AD).

Nero's persecution was unrelenting, as both Peter and Paul were victims of his cruelty. Peter by crucifixion (upside down, not deeming himself worthy to die as Christ had), and Paul, by beheading.[56]   Just two years after these brutalities Rome destroyed Jerusalem, in 70 AD.

The apostle John, however, managed to survive, and authored his Epistles, **I II, & III John** (80-85 AD), and later, while exiled on the island of Patmos, he wrote the **Revelation of Jesus Christ** (85-95 AD).

Conclusion

The persecution of the church had been as severe as her growth had been magnificent. The young church would continue her growth and her struggles even until today, as she enjoys the Promise, awaiting her hope, while Israel will soon begin to look for the fulfillment of the Promises, and the arrival of her King.

James   48 AD

	1:1	Greeting
	In Trials 1:2-20	1:2-4 Joy & Purpose in Trials
		1:5-8 Wisdom in Trials
		1:9-11 High Position in Trials
		1:12 Perseverance & Prize of Trials
		1:13-20 Trials of Temptation & Sin
James (Jacob) : New Covenant Conduct	In Action 1:21-5:19	1:21-27 Be a Doer of the Word
		2:1-13 Be Impartial
		2:14-26 Be Faithful: Demonstrate Works
		3:1-12 Be Pure of Tongue
		3:13-18 Be Wise
		4:1-12 Sources of Dissension
		4:13-17 Condemnation of the Proud
		5:1-6 Condemnation of the Wealthy
		5:7-11 Be Patient
		5:12 Do Not Swear
		5:13-18 Empathy & Prayer
		5:19 Restoring Sinners

Personal Promises

Provision of Wisdom in Trials ------------------------James 1:5
The Crown of Life --James 1:12
The Blessing For the Doer-----------------------------James 1:25
God Will Draw Near ------------------------------------James 4:8
God Will Exalt the Humble---------------------------James 4:10

Background

The name of the Epistle is Greek *Iakobou* (of Jacob). The Hebrew name was *ya'aqov*. In Latin the name was translated James (some have suggested, that this was in deference to King James the 'authorizer' of the 1611 translation, and while this is possible, there was certainly precedent for the natural translating of Jacob as James). Although the author's proper name was Jacob, he will here be referred to as James, in light of popular identification. Two men with such names are possible considerations for authorship of the Epistle: James the brother of John, who was the first apostle murdered, by Herod in 44 AD (Acts 12:2), and James the son of Joseph, and half-brother of Jesus, referred to by Paul as an apostle (Galatians 1:19), who lived until about 62 AD

The Epistle appears to have been written shortly before the Council of Jerusalem of 49 AD (Acts 15) [Note in particular the absence of any mention of Gentile believers (something to be expected after 50 AD)], and also certainly before the destruction of Jerusalem (70 AD). And it is most commonly concluded that it was the half-brother of Jesus who wrote the Letter.

Referred to by Eusebius as James the Righteous (or Just),[57] he was at first an unbeliever (John 7:5), but later came to a saving belief in Christ. He saw the resurrected Lord (I Cor. 15:5,7), which led to his being present in the upper room (Acts1:14). Later considered as an apostle (Gal. 1:19), by all accounts he became the leader of the church at Jerusalem. His leadership is evidenced in the Council of Jerusalem (Acts 15).

While the Epistle was accepted by some as authoritative, others questioned the Epistle's authority, primarily due to misunderstandings of James' explanation regarding faith and works (James 2:14-26). Eusebius, for example, included it in his antilegomena (questioned books), yet he quoted 4:11 as Scripture[58]. It was universally accepted by the church as canonical at the Third Council of Carthage.

Summary

James deals at length with the conduct of the believer, particularly in light of trials and affliction. His treatise on faith and works (2:14-26) compliments the doctrines presented by Paul, for example, and gives a full and beautiful perspective of the results of saving faith. Also, of particular note in the Epistle are the profound personal promises God makes within the book, reflecting (in very Jewish nature) that the Covenant Keeping God who guards a nation, also guards and guides his individual children, and makes promises to them that He keeps.

I Thessalonians   50 AD

Application of the Gospel	Reception of the Gospel	Standing Fast in the Gospel	4:1-12 To Self, Brothers, & Outsiders	4:13-18 The Rapture	5:1-5 The Day of the Lord (2nd Coming)	5:6-28 The Responsibility of Hope
1	2	3				

Past Growth			In Walk 4:1-12	In Hope 4:13-5:28		
1-3			4-5	Future Growth		

I Thessalonians: New Covenant Growth

Key Issue

The Hope of the Church:
The Rapture---------------------------------I Thessalonians 4:13-18

Background

Paul (with Silvanus and Timothy) wrote his earliest epistle, I Thessalonians, during his Second Missionary Journey, from Corinth in 50-51 AD (Acts 18:1-11). Paul founded the church at Thessalonica earlier in the Journey, but was forced to leave the city (Acts 17:1-10, I Thess. 2:15).

Just a short time later (2:17), Paul writes to commend the church for past growth and to encourage future growth.

Content

Paul commends the Thessalonians for their growth noting their "work of faith and labor of love and steadfastness of hope" (1:3), noting that they were already an example to the brethren (1:7). He expresses gratitude for their reception of his ministry in spite of opposition (2:14-15) at Thessalonica.

Even though the young church had proved faithful to that point, Paul encourages them to "excel still more" (4:1).

I Thessalonians 4:13-18
The Hope of the Church: The Rapture

As further encouragement, Paul presents a doctrine of hope and comfort   (4:13,18). He presents what is commonly referred to as the rapture. The term is the Latin translation of the phrase 'caught up' in v. 17, and refers to Christ receiving the church to Himself (as promised in John 14:1-3). Christ would descend, and the believers (the risen dead first) would meet him in the clouds (4:17), and would be always together with Him. This accomplishes several things:

1. Fulfills Christ's promise in John 14:1-3
2. Explains the church's absence from Revelation 4-19
3. Explains how the church returns with Christ (already being with Him) in Rev. 19.
4. Completes the understanding of the tribulation as a time of refining for Israel and judgment on the unbelieving world (Jer. 30:7, I Thess. 5:4-9).

II Thessalonians   51 AD

II Thessalonians: New Covenant Hope	1	1:1-2	Greeting
	Purpose Of Hope	1:3-5	For Growth
		1:6-10	For Assurance
		1:11	For Worthiness
		1:12	For Glory
	Clarification Of Hope 2:1-12	2:1-3	Avoid Deception of False Hope
		2:4-12	The Pure Hope: The Day of the Lord (2nd Coming)
	Provision Of Hope 2:13-3:5	2:13-14	Calling of God
		2:15-17	Standing in God
		3:1-5	Faithfulness of God
	Defense Of Hope 3:6-18	3:6	Separation From Those Without Hope
		3:7-11	Recognizing Those Without Hope
		3:12	Rebuking Those Without Hope
		3:13	Acting in Pure Hope: Be Not Weary
		3:14-15	Be Loving To Those Without Hope
		3:16-18	Benediction

Background & Content

Paul had written in I Thessalonians to encourage the believers and give them a new hope, that of the rapture. Evidently, some in the church anticipated that the promised day of the Lord (tribulation & 2nd Coming) was currently underway. Paul writes II Thessalonians less than a year later (51 AD, also from Corinth) to combat the error (2:2-3) , explaining the events that would accompany that day (2:3-12), and encouraging the saints to strength and purity.

I Corinthians　　　　54 AD

I Corinthians: New Covenant Unity	1:1-9	Commendation
	1:10-17	Corinthian Problem: Disunity
	1:18-2:16	Humility: Godly Wisdom
	3-4:5	The Corinthian Problem: Walking Fleshly –Improper Judgment
	4:6-21	The Corinthian Problem: Arrogance
	5:1-8	The Corinthian Problem: Immorality
	5:9-6:11	Proper Judgment: Judging Within The Church
	6:12-20	Morality: Glorify God in Your Body
	7	Morality: Regarding Marriage, Condition, & Priority
	8	Humility: Christian Liberty & Food
	9	Humility: Examples of Christian Liberty
	10:1-13	Morality: Example of Immorality: Israel
	10:14-33	Proper Judgment & Humility: Matters of Conscience
	11:1-16	Proper Judgment & Humility: Headship
	11:17-34	The Corinthian Problem: The Lord's Supper Misused
	12-14	Proper Judgment & Humility: Spiritual Gifts & Love
	15	Motivation & Provision For Righteousness: Resurrection
	16	General Instructions & Conclusion

Key Issue

The Hope of the Church: The Rapture --------I Cor. 15:50-58

Background

Corinth was the political capitol of Achaia, and a major trade center. The immorality of the city was legendary, and the name of the city was synonymous with moral depravity[59]

Paul first visited the city during his Second Missionary Journey (Acts 18:1), and it was there that he met Aquilla and Priscilla, whom he stayed with and worked with while he ministered in Corinth for a year and a half (Acts 18:2-3,11).

Paul was able to observe the cultural problems that the young church in Corinth faced, and a short time later, from Ephesus (I Cor. 16:8), during his Third Missionary Journey (Acts 19), Paul writes I Corinthians (54 AD), encouraging the church to maintain unity and purity under difficult circumstances.

Content

Paul alludes to a previous letter he had sent instructing them on maintaining morality amidst the Corinthian culture (5:9). The response was not as he had hoped, as he was informed of significant errors in the church to which he responded, including: disunity (1:10-17), arrogance (4:18), immorality (5:1-2), misuse of the Lord's Supper (11:28-30), and to a degree, misuse of spiritual gifts (12-14). Paul corrects these errors with pure doctrine on unity, humility, morality, and proper judgment – highlighted by his explanation of the superiority of love (13).

I Corinthians 15:50-58
The Hope of the Church: The Rapture

Here Paul reveals a 'mystery' (that which is previously not revealed). The doctrine of the rapture was not new (John 14:1-3; I Thess. 4:13-18), but the teaching of transformation to imperishable was. God's plan for imperishable bodies for believers via the rapture is identified here.

II Corinthians   55 AD

II Corinthians: New Covenant Ministers	Success	1:1-11	Comfort In Affliction
		1:12-24	Co-Workers In Christ
		2	Restoration & Forgiveness of Offending Brother
		3-4:15	Apostolic Ministry of the Gospel
		4:16-5:19	Eternal Significance of the Ministry
		5:20-6:18	Ministry of Reconciliation: Righteousness
		7	Ministry of Comfort
	Glory	8-9	Generosity in Ministry
	Opposition	10	Authority of the Ministers
		11-12:13	Authority of the Ministers: Paul
		12:14-13:14	Preparation for the Minister: Paul's Visit

Background & Content

Paul wrote II Corinthians (55 AD) from Macedonia, shortly after leaving Ephesus during his Third Missionary Journey (II Cor. 2:12; Acts 20).

He writes (1-7) to share his rejoicing over the Corinthian response to the rebukes of I Corinthians (2:1-11), and the arrival of Titus at Macedonia, and the encouraging news he brought regarding the Corinthian church (2:13; 7:5,6).

Also Paul wrote of the glory of the ministry (8-9), as he had witnessed the blossoming of the Macedonian church and the gracious gifts of the churches for the poor in Jerusalem (I Cor. 16:1; Rom. 15:25-26).

Paul concludes in 10-13 by dealing with a minority of Jews (11:22) who opposed his leadership.

Galatians   56 AD

Galatians: New Covenant Freedom	The Introduction 1:1-5	1:1-3 Prologue
		1:4-5 Praise
	The Different Gospel 1:6-2:21	1:6-7 Problem Stated
		1:8-9 Problem Condemned
		1:10-2:14 Problem Unfolded
		2:15-21 Problem Refuted
	The Doctrine 3-4	3:1-5 Error: Salvation By Flesh
		3:6-4:7 Correction: Salvation By Faith
		4:8-21 Error: Works By Law
		4:22-31 Correction: Works By Liberty
	The Duty 5-6	5:1-15 Stand In Liberty
		5:16-6:18 Walk In the Spirit

Key Issue

The Economy of the Church ---------------------Galatians 3-4

Background

Paul (1:1) addresses this epistle to the churches of the Roman province of Galatia (1:2), which was primarily gentile but did have a large Jewish population.[60] Paul, with Barnabas, had established churches in this region during the First Missionary Journey (Acts 13:4; 14:19-21). He visited the region during his Second Journey (Acts 16:6), and again in his Third (Acts 18:23).

While it is possible that Galatians was written from Antioch in 48 AD (and thus making it the earliest of Paul's epistles), it seems more likely that it was written from Ephesus in 56 AD.[61]

Content

The Galatian churches had fallen into the same error that the Judaizers of Jerusalem had eight years earlier. The basic premise in these churches of adherence to Mosaic Law and salvation by works brought a very stern rebuke from Paul:

> I am amazed that you are so quickly deserting Him who called you by the grace of Christ, for a different gospel...even though we, or an angel from heaven should preach to you a gospel contrary to that which we have preached to you, let him be accursed...You foolish Galatians, who has bewitched you... (1:6,8; 3:1)

Paul asserts his apostleship and authority, recalling past controversies on the issue of works vs. faith (2) as he prepares to reiterate the true economy of the church.

Galatians 3-4
The Economy of the Church

Paul reminds the Galatians that the Abrahamic promises (Gen 12:1-3) were not nullified by the Mosaic Covenant

(Gal. 3:15-18). He explains that the Law (being a conditional covenant) did not contradict the promises of God, but rather it served to shut up all men under sin, in order that the need for salvation by faith would be acknowledged (3:19-27), to serve as a tutor, leading men to Christ (3:24), that the promise of faith (Jer. 31; I John 2:25) might be given, and justification would be provided (3:24). Salvation came by faith, not by works, and therefore, the walk and ultimate perfection of the believer is based also upon faith, and not works (3:2).

This saving faith created a new family economy, allowing believers to be sons of God (3:26), to be united in Christ (3:28), to be heirs of promise (3:39; I John 2:25), and to be free in Christ (4).

Paul encourages the Galatians, as a result, to walk in the Spirit, and not according to the flesh (5:16), which would prove to be the only way the believer can bear true fruit (5:22-24).

Unity and humility would be the result of obedience, and upon the obedient would rest peace and mercy (6:16).

Romans   57 AD

Romans: The Gospel of Righteousness	The Message 1:1-17	1:1-7	The Gospel Promised
		1:8-15	The Gospel Preached
		1:16-17	The Gospel Defined
	The Need 1:18-3:20	1:18-32	For the Gentile
		2:1-3:8	For the Jew
		3:9-20	For All
	The Provision 3:21-4:25	3:21-31	By Faith
		4	Examples of Faith
	The Result: For Believers 5-8	5-6	Free From Penalty of Sin
		7	Free From Power of Sin
		8	Free From Presence of Sin
	The Result: For Israel 9-11	9	God is Righteous
		10	Israel Was Unrighteous
		11	God's Plan For Israel
	The Responsibility 12-15:13	12:1-2	To God
		12:3-21	To Men
		13:1-7	To Authority
		13:8-14	To Neighbors
		14-15:4	To Weaker Brother
		15:5-13	To Unity
	The Progress 15:14-16:27	15:14-33	Minister of the Gospel
		16:1-16	Servants of the Gospel
		16:17-20	Servants of Deception
		16:21-27	Conclusion

Key Prophetic Issue

The Timeline Gap --Romans 9-11

Authorship

In typical Pauline fashion, Paul states his authorship at the outset, and while he identifies himself as the author he also attributes the authority of his words directly to God. He wrote the Epistle to the Romans probably from Corinth in 56-57 AD.

In dating the Epistle, note Romans 15:25-26, which indicates that Paul was on his way from Macedonia and Achaia, heading to Jerusalem.

> Paul was about to go to Jerusalem...and planned to take along contributions from believers in Macedonia and Achaia...This clearly refers to the famous collection that Paul sponsored during his third Journey.[62]

This collection is referenced in I Cor. 16, and again in II Cor. 8. In the latter reference, Macedonia had already made their contribution. At the time of the writing of Romans, the Corinthians also had given (Achaia being the province in which Corinth was located). Paul would return to Jerusalem to end his Third Missionary Journey. In Jerusalem Paul was arrested and began his imprisonment. At the time Romans was written, Paul was a free man. Therefore the Epistle was written sometime during the end of his Third Missionary Journey. Romans 16:1-2 references Phoebe, and implies that she was the carrier of the letter. She was from the church at Cenchrea (a southern suburb of Corinth). It is most likely that Paul wrote the Epistle during his last visit to Corinth.

The Epistle is really the chief part of the New Testament and the very purest gospel, and it is worthy not only that every Christian should know it word for word, by heart, but occupy himself with it every day, as the daily bread of the soul. It can never be read or pondered too much, and the more it is dealt with the more precious it becomes, and the better it tastes.[63]

-Martin Luther

Purpose

Paul wrote the Epistle as a substitute for his presence. He expressed a strong desire to be present with the believers in Rome but realizing the impracticality of being in Rome, he wrote a letter communicating the very things he longed to communicate to them in person. Unlike several other Pauline epistles Paul does not write with the purpose of correcting any particular problem – there is no particular failure of the Roman church that Paul addresses. Rather he sought to "preach the gospel" (1:15), even to those who were already believers in Rome. He emphasizes that the need for the hearing and understanding of the gospel does not end once a man is saved; rather it only just begins, for the gospel is *the* way of life.

Summary

Right away, Paul states the thesis of the epistle:

For I am not ashamed of the gospel, for it is the power of God for salvation to everyone who believes, to the Jew first and also to the Greek. For in it the righteousness of God is revealed from faith to faith; as it is written, 'but the righteous man shall live by faith.' (1:17)

In 1-3:20 Paul acknowledges man's need for salvation, emphasizing in particular the total depravity of man, and the fact that all men are without excuse and stand condemned.

In 3:21-4:25 he provides the solution for the problem, namely salvation by faith through Jesus Christ. Paul hones in on Abraham as the example of faith, bringing to our memory God's promise to Abraham that through him all the families of the earth would be blessed (Gen. 12:3). Again, the promises of God are in full view, and His work in fulfilling them is the crux of the New Testament.

In chapters 5-8 he deals with the results of salvation, specifically freedom from the penalty, power, and ultimately presence of sin.

Paul explains the big picture for Israel in 9-11, demonstrating God's purpose and redemptive work with Israel, and the keeping of His promises. In doing so, he identifies the purpose of the church as she relates to Israel and explains indirectly the timeline gap of Daniel 9.

And finally, 12-16 gives a very detailed exposition of the application of righteousness in daily living for the believer.

Romans 9-11
The Timeline Gap

In light of the promises made to the believer in 8:28-39, Paul addresses the seemingly delayed promises that God made to Israel, asserting that "it is not as though the word of God has failed" (9:6), recalling that God's promises were based upon His sovereignty (9:14-18), Paul explains that God had brought righteousness by faith to the gentiles as well (10), and that Israel had been hardened by God (11:7-10), resulting in a temporary setting aside of the nation in order that the opportunity for salvation would come to the gentiles (11:25, aka, the times of the gentiles, Luke 21:24).

This is the gap in Daniel's 490 year timeline (Dan. 9), which came in between the 483rd and 484th year. This gap indicates an even broader scope of the promises of God than many imagined. God had a dual purpose in saving the believing gentiles, (1) the obvious result was their salvation, and (2) their belief would result in a jealousy on the part of the Jews, resulting in their own turning to Messiah, which would bring their salvation (11:13-15).

God in His splendid plan would keep His promises to Abraham by restoring Israel through Abraham's descendants (who were his descendants both physical and spiritual), and His promise to Abraham of blessing on the nations, by the forgiveness of sins through the righteousness that comes through faith.

Philippians   61 AD

Philippians: Walking With God Despite Affliction	Circumstances In Affliction 1	1:1-2 Greeting
		1:3-11 Philippians' Circumstances
		1:12-26 Paul's Circumstances
		1:27-29 Encouragement In Circumstances
	Unity In Affliction 2	2:1-11 Unity by Humility
		2:12-18 Unity by Holiness
		2:19-30 Unity by Concern
	Perseverance In Affliction 3	3:1-16 Perspective of Perseverance
		3:17-21 Prize of Perseverance
	Peace In Affliction 4	4:1-3 Peace With Brethren
		4:4-9 Peace With God
		4:10-20 Peace With Circumstances
		4:21-23 Conclusion

Background

The city of Philippi was a "leading city of the district of Macedonia" (Acts 16:12).

It has been called "Rome in miniature"[64], as its peoples were Roman citizens, possessing the privilege to vote, and had their own governing senate and legislature[65].

Paul first journeyed there with Timothy and Silas (Acts 16:3) during his Second Missionary Journey, staying for some days, and speaking to women who had assembled outside the city (Acts 16:12-13). It was here that Paul met Lydia from Thyatira, who became the first Christian in Europe (Acts 16:14-15). Paul and Silas were later imprisoned there for casting out a demon from a girl who was very profitable in fortune telling (Acts 16:16-24). The two were miraculously freed, resulting in the salvation of the jailor and his household (Acts 16:27-34). Paul also visited during his Third Missionary Journey (Acts 20:6).

Paul wrote this epistle during his first imprisonment in Rome (1:13; 4:22) around 61 AD, along with Ephesians, Colossians, and Philemon, which were written soon after.

Content

Paul expresses the bitterness of his imprisonment, yet the epistle is filled with gratitude and contentment. He thanks the Philippians for their contributions while he was at Thessalonica (4:16) and Corinth (II Cor. 11:8-9), and encourages them to stand firm in spite of opposition (1:15-17; 27-28). He challenges them to unity, humility, and perseverance, reminding them of the examples of Christ (2:1-11), Timothy (2:19-30), and himself (2:12-18; 3). Paul's challenges were brought on, in part, by disunity reported among key women in the church (4:2-3).

He concludes the epistle with an earnest call to prayer (4:6), peace (4:7), purity (4:8-9), and contentment through the strength of Christ (4:10-13).

Paul trusted in the Covenant Keeping God even when the covenant keeping was not so evident.

Philemon 63 AD

Philemon: New Covenant Repentance & Forgiveness	1-3		Greeting & Introduction
	Commendation of Philemon 4-7	4-5	For Love & Faith
		6	For Faith
		7	For Love
	Plea for Onesimus 8-10	8-9	The Nature of the Plea
		10	The Object of the Plea
	Usefulness of Onesimus 11-18	11	Once Useful
		12-15	Now Useful: As Minister
		16	Now Useful: As Brother
		17-18	Now Useful: As Partner
	Final Plea of Paul 19-22	19-21	For Onesimus
		22	For Lodging
	23-25		Conclusion

Background & Content

Writing during the latter part of his first Roman imprisonment (63 AD), Paul commends Philemon (a Colossian believer who owed his life to Paul, v.19) for his love of the saints and his faith in the Lord (4). He reminds Philemon that he could order him to do right, but makes a loving appeal instead (8-9). Paul's appeal is on behalf of his 'child' in the faith (10), Onesimus, a native of Colossae (Col. 4:9), and a servant of Philemon, who, seeking his freedom ran away to Rome, but instead found true freedom in Christ through the ministry of Paul during his imprisonment in Rome. Paul requests that Philemon receives him back, not as a slave, but as a brother (16). Paul sends Onesimus with this letter in hand (along with the epistle to the Colossians, Col. 4:9), addressed not only to Philemon, but also to Apphia, Archippus, and the church (1:2).

The letter serves as a reminder that New Covenant forgiveness is to be given, just as it is to be received (Matt. 18:21-35).

Ephesians 63 AD

Ephesians: New Covenant Wealth	The Position Of the Believer 1-3	1:1-14	Basis: Father Son & Holy Spirit
		1:15-23	Prayer for Understanding
		2:1-10	New Life
		2:11-22	New Peace
		3:1-13	New Administration
		3:14-20	New Power
	The Walk Of the Believer 4-6	4:1-16	In Unity
		4:17-24	In Newness
		4:25-32	In Truth
		5:1-14	In Love & Righteousness
		5:15-20	In Wisdom
		In Subjection 5:21-6:9 — 5:21	The Basis: Fear of Christ
		5:22-23	Wives & Husbands
		6:1-4	Children & Parents
		6:5-9	Servants & Masters
		6:10-17	In Strength
		6:18-20	In Prayer
		6:21-23	In Peace & Grace

Key Prophetic Issues

Background

Paul wrote the Epistle to the Ephesians in 63 AD, during his first imprisonment in Rome. He addressed the Letter to "the saints who are at Ephesus and those who are faithful in Christ Jesus" (1:1). The Epistle to the Ephesians, along with Colossians and Philemon were circulated between the churches in a rough geographical circle. Typically referred to as encyclical letters, due to the manner of their circulation, they were hand carried by Tychicus (6:21)

Note that some of the ancient manuscripts do not contain the words "at Ephesus" in verse 1, and due to this, it is suggested by some that the audience of the Epistle was more general. Paul tells the Colossians to expect an epistle from the church at Laeodicea (Col. 4:16), an almost certain reference to the Epistle to the Ephesians.

Ephesus is first mentioned in Acts 18-19, and the church there was probably founded by Aquila, Priscilla, and Paul, as he reasoned with the Jews in the synagogue (18:19). Paul later returned to Ephesus, and finding faithful disciples there he continued to teach and perform miracles for two years. Ephesus' young and thriving church was challenged by the culture of the city, which was a commercial hub of Asia Minor, with much of the commerce revolving around the worship (i.e., selling of crafted idols, cultic prostitution, etc.) of the Ephesian false goddess Artemis (or Diana in Latin). Revelation 2:1-7 indicates that the Ephesian church ultimately did not heed the exhortations of Paul in his Epistle, as Jesus said that the church had left its first love.

Summary

Paul does not rebuke the church for any wrongdoing; rather his purpose is to clarify the position of the believer and to challenge the believer to walk in a manner worthy of that position.

The first 3 chapters explain in detail the basis and character of the believer's position, while the last 3 chapters deal with the applications of these doctrines. In typical Pauline form, the theology comes first, and then the call to action.

Ephesians 1:3
The Scope of the Church

The key identifier of the true scope of the church is found here:

> Blessed be the God and Father of our Lord Jesus Christ who has blessed us with every spiritual blessing in the heavenlies in Christ. (1:3)

There are two key descriptions:
1. *The blessings of the church are spiritual.*
This is in direct contrast to many of Israel's covenant blessings. While there is no doubt that the believer will share in some earthly blessings (particularly during the Millennium), the blessings of the church are decidedly not physical. The gospel is not a gospel of 'health and wealth'; it is a message of spiritual life for the believer.
Also note that the believer possesses every spiritual blessing. Tremendous riches indeed.

2. *The spiritual blessings are described as being 'in the heavenlies in Christ'.*
The focal point of the church is heaven not earth. It is the spiritual not the physical. Contrasting once again with the covenant promises to Israel that focus on the earth.

The basis for possessing and inheriting these blessings is (like God's unconditional covenant promises to Israel) completely dependent upon the grace of God:

> For by grace you have been saved through faith, and that not of yourselves, it is the gift of God that no one should boast. For we are His workmanship, created for good works, which God prepared beforehand that we should walk in them. (2:8-10)

Ephesians 3:1-6; 5:28-32
The Mystery of the Church

Mystery is from the Greek *musterion*, and it refers not to the enigmatic, but to that which has previously been unrevealed. These passages reveal two mystery aspects of the church:

1. "there was made known to me the mystery...that the Gentiles are fellow heirs and fellow members of the body, and fellow partakers of the promise in Christ Jesus through the Gospel." (3:3, 6)

Gentiles have joint participation, (not in the covenant promises, but in the covenant promise) specifically participation in the body of Christ and the promise through the gospel. What is that promise? Eternal life (I John 2:25)

This is a concept that was vaguely alluded to in Genesis 12:3 – "through you all the families of the earth shall be blessed", and here we see the continuing fulfillment of God's promise to Abraham.

2. In regard to the marital relationship of man and woman, Paul says

> this mystery is great; but I am speaking with reference to Christ and the church. (5:32)

The marital relationship is an illustration of Christ's relationship to the church. This points us to Revelation 19:7, which says,

> Let us rejoice and be glad and give glory to Him, for the marriage of the Lamb has come and His bride has made herself ready.

The church is pictured as betrothed to Christ in the current age. Christ gave Himself up for her in the ultimate act of love. The marriage is referred to in the past tense in Revelation 19:7 (by the use of the aorist tense of *elthen*, translated, is come), therefore the ceremonial marriage seems to take place at the rapture of the church (I Thess. 4:13-18), and is celebrated at His 2nd Coming. The church is there described as being clothed in fine linen and clean (Rev. 19:7,14). Note God's efficacious work in perfecting the church. The bride is to respond to Him by submitting to His love (Eph. 5:22-33).

Colossians 63 AD

Colossians: Walking In the Knowledge of the All Sufficient Christ

Christ is Sufficient for Salvation 1-2:7			1:1-8	Acceptance of the Gospel
			1:9-12	Walk In the Gospel Desired & Explained
			1:13-23	Substance of the Gospel: Christ
			1:24-29	Minister of the Gospel: Paul
			2:1-7	Walk in the Gospel Commanded
Christ is Sufficient for Growth 2:8-23			2:8-10	As Opposed to Philosophies
			2:11-17	As Opposed to Law
			2:18-19	As Opposed to False Doctrine
			2:20-23	As Opposed to Self Made Religion
Christ is Sufficient for Our Walk 3-4:6	Mind		3:1-4	Seek Things Above
	Manner		3:5-7	Consider the Old Man Dead
			3:8-9	Lay Aside the Old Man
			3:10-11	Put on the New Man
		Characteristics of the New Man — Gen.	3:12-17	Of Believers
		Specific	3:18	Of Wives
			3:19	Of Husbands
			3:20	Of Children
			3:21	Of Fathers
			3:22-25	Of Servants
			4:1	Of Masters
			4:2-4	In Prayer
			4:5-6	In Witness
Servants of Christ 4:7-18			4:7-9	Coming of Servants
			4:10-18	Commendation of Servants

Background

Colossae was a trade center in Phrygia, roughly twelve miles north of Laodicea. Paul apparently never visited Colossae of Laodicea (2:1), and it is best to conclude that the church was founded by Epaphras (1:7; 4:12).

Along with Philippians, Philemon, and Ephesians, Paul wrote this epistle during his imprisonment in Rome (63 AD) (4:4, 10, 18).

The epistle was an encyclical, meaning that it was to be circulated among the churches, specifically to Laodicea, from whom was coming to the Colossians another encyclical epistle, probably the epistle to the Ephesians (4:15-16). This letter was hand carried by Tychichus and Onesimus (4:7,9).

Content

The book closely parallels the epistle to the Ephesians, covering much of the same material, but with a more Christological focus.

Paul reveals the *mystery* of the Person of Christ: His identity and majesty (2:2; 4:3), and His ministry indwelling believers (1:26-27). Paul also emphasizes the importance of the battle for the mind of the Christian in understanding the Person of Christ (1:10; 2:2-3, 8, 18; 3:1-2). A proper perspective of the Person of Jesus Christ will allow for a proper walk (1:9-10) while a misunderstanding of Who He is can result in only inconsistency and fleshly living (2:8, 23).

Paul demonstrates in the instructional section of the book the sufficiency of Christ for the believer's salvation (1:13-23), and for his growth (2:8-23). The deity of Christ is boldly asserted (1:13-20).

The second half of the epistle addresses the application of the doctrine presented in chapters 1 and 2, emphasizing Christ as the sufficiency for the believer's walk (3-4).

I Timothy

65 AD

I Timothy: New Covenant Godliness	Charge to Godliness	1:1-2	Greetings
		1:3-4	Promote Godliness
		1:5-11	Purpose
	1:1-20	1:12-17	Patience
		1:18-20	Perseverance
	Desirability Of Godliness	2:1-7	As a Testimony
		2:8	In Men
	2-3:13	2:9-15	In Women
		3:1-13	In Leaders
	Explanation of Godliness	3:14-15	The Household of God
		3:16	The Basis: The Ministry
	3:14-4:16	4:1-6	The Opposition
		4:7-16	The Defense
	Practice of Godliness	5:1	In Regard to Men
		5:2	In Regard to Women
		5:3-16	In Regard to Widows
		5:17-25	In Regard to Elders, Ailments, & Sin
		6:1-2	In Regard to Servants & Masters
		6:3-5	In Regard to Sound Doctrine
		6:6-10	In Regard to Money & Contentment
	5-6:21	6:11-21	In Regard to Timothy

Background

Timothy is introduced as a well spoken of disciple from Lystra, whose mother was a Jewish believer, and whose father was apparently a Greek unbeliever (Acts 16:1).

Paul brought Timothy with him on the Second and Third Missionary Journeys (Acts16:3; 19:22; 20:4). Timothy's presence with Paul throughout Paul's ministry is often acknowledged throughout the epistles. Through their ministering together, Paul developed a strong bond of friendship with him, even referring to him as his son in the faith (1:2, 18; II Tim. 1:2). Timothy served as the leader of the church in Ephesus.

Timothy knew firsthand of Paul's hardships, even being imprisoned himself just before the book of Hebrews was written (Heb. 13:23).

Paul writes this epistle after his release from his first imprisonment in Rome (3:14-15), probably 65 AD. It is the first of his three pastoral epistles to the two young leaders (Timothy and Titus) who had served in the ministry with Paul.

Content

Paul encourages Timothy to remain at Ephesus in order to combat false teaching (1:3-11), and to persevere, fighting the good fight (1:18). He provides Timothy with the outlines for maintaining personal godliness, as well as godliness in relation to the ministry of the church.

Even though Timothy was an impressively mature young leader in the church, Paul cautions him to flee from the things which bring about ungodliness (6:3-16), and to guard the stewardship that God had given to Timothy (6:20-21; II Tim. 1:14).

Purity and humility are the characteristics of a godly leader. Guarding those characteristics will keep that leader from going astray (6:21).

Titus   65 AD

Titus: New Covenant Purity	Salutation **1:1-4**	1:1	Writer: Paul
		1:2-3	Basis of Writing: The Promise
		1:4	Recipient: Titus
	Battle For Purity **1:5-16**	1:5-9	Defense of Purity: Elders
		1:10-16	Attack on Purity: False Teachers
	Duty Of Purity **2-3:11**	2:1	Of Titus
		2:2	Of Older Men
		2:3	Of Older Women
		2:4-5	Of Younger Women
		2:6	Of Young Men
		2:7-8	Of Titus
		2:9-10	Of Servants
		2:11-14	The Motive: Grace
		2:15	Of Titus
		3:1-2	Of All Men & Women
		3:3-7	The Motive: Grace
		3:8-11	Of Titus
	Conclusion **3:12-15**	3:12	Appeal for Visit
		3:13	Appeal for Help
		3:14	Appeal for Giving
		3:15	Final Greetings

Background

Titus apparently was first associated with Paul at Antioch and traveled with Paul and Barnabus to Jerusalem (Gal. 2:1,3; Acts 15).

Paul expresses disappointment at not having opportunity to meet Titus in Troas (II Cor. 2:13), but the two later joined up in Macedonia (II Cor. 7:6-7; 13-15). Paul sent him to Corinth to assist with the collection for the saints of Jerusalem (II Cor 8:6, 16-24). Later, Titus was left in Crete (1:5) to fulfill the same function there as Timothy in Ephesus. As he did for Timothy, Paul cared a great deal for Titus, affectionately referring to Titus as his 'true child in a common faith' (1:4).

Paul wrote to Titus during approximately the same time he wrote his first epistle to Timothy, during a brief period of freedom in between his imprisonments in Rome, probably in 65 AD, during a time when he planned to go to Nicopolis (3:12).

Content

Paul writes to Titus acknowledging the promise of eternal life from ages past, which is revealed in Christ (1:1-3). His purpose is to encourage Titus to maintain personal purity, and purity in the church, in order to defeat the false doctrine of those who were disobedient and licentious (1:10-16). As in his letter to Timothy, Paul instructs on the duties of believers in the church, and the order to be maintained.

Paul closes with a request that Titus make an effort to visit him in Nicopolis (Paul would send Artemis or Tychichus to fill in while he was away) (3:12), and that he assist Zenas, the lawyer, and Apollos in their coming to Crete (3:13).

II Timothy 67-68 AD

II Timothy: New Covenant Conduct	1:1-2	Greeting
	1:3-5	Paul's Fondness of Timothy
	1:6-14	Paul's Encouragement of Timothy
	1:15-18	Commendation of Onesipherus
	2:1-3	Paul's Fatherly Entreaty: Be Strong
	2:4-13	Examples: Soldier, Farmer, Christ
	2:14-26	Paul's Charge to Timothy: Required Conduct
	3:1-13	Warning of the Last Days
	3:14-4:8	Paul's Solemn Charge: Preach the Word
	4:9-22	Final Instructions

Background & Content

Shortly after Paul's first letters to Timothy and Titus, he was imprisoned again in Rome. His second letter to Timothy, and his final epistle, is written toward the latter part of his imprisonment probably in 67-68 AD. In the letter Paul expresses personal suffering on behalf of the gospel (1:12), and his abandonment (1:15; 4:16), as only Luke had remained by his side (4:11). He recognizes that his end was fast approaching (4:6), and his simple requests for comfort included his cloak, books, and parchments (4:13). He hopes to see Timothy one last time (4:18), but offers him final instructions anyway.

Even amidst the seeming hopelessness of Paul's situation, he draws comfort in his confidence in the promises of God through the gospel (1:12), and in the awareness that he had served faithfully and would be rewarded in accordance with those promises (4:7-8).

He encourages Timothy to be diligent in his ministry (2; 4:1-8), and warns him of coming apostasy (3). And, probably just a few months later, Paul was martyred.

He proved faithful to the Promises of God, and an example to young believers such as Timothy and Titus.

Hebrews   64-67 AD

Hebrews: Majesty of the Son	1-10:18	Understanding The Son	1-2	Position of the Son
			3	Faithfulness of the Son: Superior to Moses
			4:1-13	Rest of the Son
			4:14-5:10	Priesthood of the Son: Superior to Aaron
			5:11-6:12	Maturity in the Son
			6:13-7:28	Priesthood of the Son: The Order of Melchizedek
			8	Ministry of the Son: New Covenant
			9-10:18	Sacrifice of the Son: The Perfect Offering
	10:19-13:25	Pleasing The Son	10:19-39	Confidence in the Son: Sacrifice For Sins
			11-12:3	Faith in the Son: Examples
			12:4-11	Discipline in the Son
			12:12-13:25	Walking in the Son

Authorship

The authorship of Hebrews is not known (by man) for certain, and there are numerous opinions as to who was the most likely candidate.

Early Views:

Clement of Alexandria believed that Paul wrote it in Hebrew and that Luke translated it into Greek. Origen viewed it as Paul's work, but recognized it to have a different quality than Paul's usual style, also considering later the possibility of Luke's involvement, but ultimately he acknowledged that no one really knows but God. The Eastern church as a whole recognized Pauline authorship, while the Western church did not. Tertullian attributed the writing to Barnabus, Martin Luther to Apollos.[66]

Athanasius convinced the Roman church to agree with the Eastern church on Pauline authorship. Eusebius quoted Hebrews as authoritative, but not Pauline.

By mid fourth century, the Roman church accepted Hebrews as authoritative. Amborse of Milan (339-397) accepted the authority of the letter, but questioned its authorship. Rufinius (345-410) saw it as Pauline. Jerome seems to have recognized Pauline authorship, however he did recognize the controversy, and importantly understood that canonicity is not depended solely on apostolic authorship. Augustine recognized it as Pauline until 406 after which time he refers to it as anonymous. The Council of Hippo (393) recognized Pauline authorship. Thomas Aquinas thought it was a Lukan translation of Paul's Hebrew original. Erasmus denied Pauline authorship, but he also denied Johannine authorship of Revelation. Martin Luther recognized it as canonical, though of secondary importance he recognized Apollos as the author. John Calvin recognized it as canonical, but not Pauline, thinking it was either written by Luke or Clement of Rome.[67]

In regard to Pauline authorship Henry says

> As to the penman of this epistle, we are not so certain it does not bear the name on any in front of it as the rest of the epistles do, and there has been some dispute among the learned to whom they should ascribe it. But it is generally ascribed to the apostle Paul. In earlier times is was generally ascribed to him.[68]

But A.T. Robertson disagrees, saying that "no early writer apparently attributed the Greek text to Paul"[69]. Robertson dates the letter as prior to the destruction of the temple in 70A.D., and he recognizes Apollos as the author.

Although there is much divergence of early opinion regarding the authorship of Hebrews, the authority of Hebrews was unmistakable, and it was held in high regard as Scripture: The Chester Beatty Papyri (mid 3rd century) contained 104 pages of Pauline epistles and included Hebrews. Codex Augensis (6th century) is a manuscript of Pauline epistles and also includes Hebrews. Codex Washingtonianus (5th century) again includes Pauline epistles with Hebrews. Codex Mosquensis (9th century) contains the same.[70]

The Probables

There are four characters who are most commonly considered as possibilities for authorship of Hebrews. They are Paul, Luke, Barnabus, and Apollos. Any other considerations would be totally speculative. An examination of the character and backgrounds of these four men can provide insight as to the likelihood of their involvement.

What does the text say of the author?

1. He does not identify himself by name, but he seems to assume his readers know him
2. He was not an eyewitness of Christ (2:3)
3. He knew of Timothy as a brother during Timothy's imprisonment (13:23)
4. He was very well versed in OT Scriptures
5. He quotes the Septuagint exclusively for OT references
6. He wrote in a superior style, an educated style of Koine Greek.

Paul does not seem to fit these characteristics. He identifies himself by name in his letters. He was an eyewitness of Christ on the road to Damascus. Whether or not Paul was alive during Timothy's imprisonment is questionable. He makes frequent use in his letters not only of the Septuagint, but also quotes the Hebrew texts of the Old Testament. The style of this letter is of distinctly higher literary quality than that of Paul's other epistles.

Considering these factors, Pauline authorship is very unlikely.

Luke has also been ascribed the author by some, with little if any evidence. In Luke's other writings, he identifies himself by name with a proper introduction. He did however fit the second criteria, as he was apparently not an eyewitness of Christ. He also would have known Timothy as a 'brother'. He was very familiar with the Old Testament, and being of Greek heritage, it would have been natural for him to quote the Septuagint. The style of this book is notably different from Luke's, as Luke was a historian, while the book of Hebrews is a theology and an exposition of the Old Testament – very Jewish in flavor. Luke could have authored Hebrews, but the lack of evidence would make this unlikely.

Barnabus is introduced as "Joseph", a Levite known as Barnabus to the apostles (Acts 4:36). He is later described as a good man, full of the Holy Spirit and full of faith (Acts 11:24). He was of Cyprian birth but apparently a resident of Jerusalem where the Hebrew texts, as opposed to the Septuagint, were read in the Synogogue. He could have fit all six characteristics, but it is not recorded, and therefore not known whether he did or not. Lack of evidence seems also to make him an improbable candidate.

Apollos is introduced as a Jew of Alexandria, an eloquent man, mighty in the Scriptures, and as a powerful speaker who demonstrated from the Scripture that Jesus was the Christ (Acts 18:24). Apollos was not an eyewitness of Christ. He did know of Timothy as a brother. He was clearly very knowledgeable in the Old Testament, being very familiar with 'the things of Jesus' (the basic theme of Hebrews). Being of Alexandrian heritage, he would have been almost exclusively familiar with the Septuagint. Also note the way in which Paul speaks of Apollos in I Corinthians. Paul explains that while he himself did the planting, Apollos did the watering (I Cor. 3:6). Apollos was a leader in the young church, and his authority was confirmed by Paul the apostle. Therefore, it seems that

Apollos more definitely fits the profile of the author of Hebrews than any of the other three most likely characters.

Importance
The important issue is not apostolic authorship (for then we would have problem with the writings of Mark, Luke, and James), rather it is apostolic authority. The author of Hebrews is obviously not an apostle, but his message was apostolic in every way. It is in complete agreement with the writings of the apostles, and it claims to be the record of God speaking through His Son (1:1-2). It is a message of undeniable authority, and any of the four individuals possessed the authority to write such a book. All possessed approval by the apostles (Paul of course being one), and all would have had the capability to be used of God to produce such a work. Therefore, although we cannot be certain of the author, we can be quite certain that the words are from the mouth of God.

Content

The author presents Jesus as the One Who was qualified to fill every role of Messiah. He was superior to every Old Testament picture that portrayed Him. He is God's final Word (1). He is the Propitiation for sin and the perfect Man (2). He is the perfect High Priest (3-7). He is the Minister of the New Covenant (8), and the fulfillment of the Old (9). He is the perfect Sacrifice (10). He is the Life Giver through faith (11), and the fulfillment of God's promises (11:39-40). All examples point to Him (12), and He remains always the same (13:8).

The author emphasizes that the identity of Jesus Christ is the key that unlocks the Promises of God. To neglect Him is to neglect the entire message of Scripture (2:1-4; John 5:39).

I Peter   65-67 AD

I Peter: New Covenant Holiness Amid Persecution	Explanation of Holiness 1:1-12	1:1	The Beginning
		1:2-9	The Basis
		1:10-12	The Bearing Witness
	Reasons For Holiness 1:13-2:12	1:13-22	Redeeming Work of Christ
		1:23-2:3	Regeneration Through the Word
		2:4-8	Relationship to Christ
		2:9-10	Reception of Mercy
		2:11-12	Righteousness Amid Persecution
	Specifics of Holiness 2:13-3:9a	2:13-18	Submit to Authority
		2:19-20	Suffer for Righteousness
		2:21-25	Suffering Example: Christ
		3:1-9a	Submit to One Another
	Motivation for Holiness 3:9b-4:19	3:9b-17	Blessing of God
		3:18-22	Bought & Baptized
		4:1-11	Because it is Time
		4:12-19	Blessing by Testing
	5:1-5		Leadership in Holiness
	5:6-11		Protection in Holiness
	5:12-14		Conclusion

Background

The Roman persecutions of the church by Nero brought grave concern to those who survived. With their very existence threatened, how were they to respond?

Peter addresses his first epistle to the believers (primarily Jewish believers of the Diaspora) who were scattered in the provinces of Asia Minor "Pontus, Galatia,

Cappadocia, Asia, and Bithynia." (1:1), and were affected by these persecutions.

Regarding Peter's audience, Tenney gives insight:

> Two of these provinces, Pontus and Cappadocia, are not mentioned in Acts among those evangelized by Paul; Bithynia he attempted to reach, but was forbidden to do so (Acts 16:7). Galatia and Asia he did evangelize...Men from Cappadocia and Pontus were present on the day of Pentecost (Acts 2:9) and may have returned to their homes with the news of the coming of the Messiah and the outpouring of the Holy Spirit.[71]

Peter states his authorship in 1:1, also identifying his location of writing as Babylon (5:13), but this is an apparent reference to Rome (Rev. 14:8; 16:19; 17:5; 18:2,10,21). The date of writing seems most likely 65–67 AD, shortly before his martyrdom.

Content

Peter writes to encourage the Jewish believers to maintain their holiness amid persecution. He first recalls the basis of positional holiness: the foreknowledge of the Father, the sanctifying of the Spirit, and the blood of Christ (1:2). Because of the authority of the basis, the outcome was assured (1:3-5). God would keep His promise through faith.

He challenges the believers to 'gird your minds for action' (1:13) and recounts the reasons for maintaining holiness, foremost of which was the Person, work, and example of Christ. (2). He includes a call to submission even to the king (2:13-20), always referring to Christ as the Example. He encourages the believers to maintain the proper attitudes (4), and not to be surprised at the persecution (12-19). He concludes by pointing out that their suffering helped serve the purpose of their own maturing, and that God would achieve His purpose in them (5:10).

II Peter   66-67 AD

II Peter: New Covenant Reminder: Be Diligent	Basis for Diligence: The Promises 1:1-4	1:1	Author of the Letter
		1:2-4	Author of the Promises
	Diligence Due To Promise 1:5-15	1:5-11	Diligence for Growth
		1:12-15	Diligence for Knowledge
	Nature of Promises 1:16-3:18	1:16-21	Promises Seen: Prophets
		2:1-3	Promises Denied: False Prophets
		2:4-10	Promise Preserved
		2:11-22	Promises Opposed
		3:1-2	Promises Remembered
		3:3-13	Promise Coming
		3:14-18	Promise Motivation: Be Diligent

Background & Content

Peter completes his earthly ministry by writing a second epistle, this one "to those who have received a faith of the same kind as ours" (1:1).

Whereas in the first letter, he is concerned with the believer's ability to deal with persecution, here he is concerned with their ability to maintain diligence in accordance with true knowledge, and to avoid the false teachings that had arisen. He seeks to be "stirring up your sincere mind by way of reminder" (3:1). And if any should doubt the assurance of the promised coming Day of the Lord, Peter reminds them that God's delaying is due to His patience, as He seeks the salvation of the lost (3:9). Probably only months after writing this epistle, Peter was crucified upside down by Nero.[72]

Jude   65-80 AD

Jude: Contend For the Faith	Threat Of the Ungodly 1-4	1-3	The Battle
		4	The Opposition
	Examples Of the Ungodly 5-7	5	Of Israel
		6	Of Angels
		7	Of Sodom & Gomorrah
	Description Of the Ungodly 8-19	8-13	They Are Wicked
		14-19	They Are Prophesied
	Action of the Godly 20-23	20-21	To Yourselves
		22-23	To the Ungodly
	Keeper Of the Godly 24-25	24	He is Able
		25	He is Sovereign

Authorship

The book of Jude was written between 65-80 A.D. to "those who are the called, beloved in God the Father, and kept for Jesus Christ" (v.1). The name Jude is another form of the name Judas, and the author identifies himself as "a bond servant of Jesus Christ, and brother of James" (v.11). The author was almost certainly either Judas the apostle (not Iscariot), or Judas the half brother of Jesus. It would seem highly unlikely that the apostle Judas penned this Letter, as the author refers to the apostles as 'they' (vv.17-18), and seemingly did not include himself in their number. It was the custom of the day to identify oneself as being the son of someone; in this case, Jude identifies himself as the brother of James – probably due to James' prominence in the church at Jerusalem, and his modesty toward his relation to Christ. And because the James being spoken of is most likely the half brother of Jesus (Mt. 13:55), it would seem most probable that the author was a half-brother of Jesus. Due to remarkable parallel in the first 18 verses of Jude with II Peter 2:3-18, some have suggested a dependence by Jude on Peter's writings, however, as illustrated by the Gospels, God can give different men similar messages in order to accomplish His purpose.

Authority

Assuming the author to be a half brother of Jesus, Jude had the same authority to write as James. He would have obviously been an eyewitness, intimately acquainted with Jesus, was (with James) in Jerusalem in the Upper Room with the disciples before Pentecost (Acts 1:14), and was almost certainly a participant in the Spirit's coming at Pentecost (Acts 2:1). The authority of Jude was questioned by some early church fathers, primarily due to Jude's quotations of extra-Biblical sources (i.e., I Enoch quoted in vv.14-15, and the Assumption of Moses quoted in v.9). It must be noted that Paul also made use of extra-Biblical sources, citing Greek writings in Acts 17:28 and Titus 1:12-13. This literary tool does not invalidate authority, and thus, appropriately Jude was accepted into the Canon of Scripture[73]

Summary

Jude's purpose in writing is stated in vv. 3-4, in which he appeals to believers that they might "contend earnestly for the faith" (v.3). In light of the promised "mercy of our Lord Jesus Christ" (v.21), he reminds believers that there is a battle for truth, and warns them of the dangers brought by false teachers and their heresies. Of great significance to the believer amidst these dangers is Jude's exhortation to respond in mercy (even if with caution) to those in danger of falling prey to error (vv.22-23).

I John   80-85 AD

I John: New Covenant Fellowship	Vertical Fellowship	1:1-4	The Basis: The Word of Life
		1:5-10	The Conditions
		2:1-2	The Advocate: Jesus Christ
		2:3-6	The Obedience
		2:7-11	The Commandment: Love
		2:12-14	The Maturity
		2:15-17	The Warning of Worldliness
		2:18-23	The Lie vs. The Truth
		2:24-29	The Promise: Eternal Life
		3:1-10	The Righteousness
	1-3	3:11-18	The Love Needed
	Horizontal Fellowship	4:1-6	The Discernment
		4:7-18	The Love Explained
		4:19-21	The Basis of Love
		5:1-5	The Belief
		5:6-12	The Witness
		5:13-15	The Assurance
	4-5	5:16-21	The Sin

Key Promise

The Promise: Eternal Life ----------------------------I John 2:25

Background

John's first epistle, in a way is an exposition of his Gospel. It is very much related in terminology and in thought.

John addresses his letter to those he calls his little children (2:1), beloved (2:7), fathers (2:13), young men

(2:13), and brethren (3:13). It could have been an encyclical letter, even sent to the same churches addressed in Revelation.[74] The most likely date seems best to be placed between 80-85 AD.

Content

His purpose for writing is succinctly stated (as it is in his Gospel) in 5:13:

> These things I have written to you who believe in the name of the Son of God, in order that you may know tht you have eternal life.

His Gospel was written to bring about belief in Christ, and his first epistle was written to bring about assurance of that belief, the evidence of which was love and Christian fellowship.

He concentrates on the vertical relationship with God through Christ in chapters 1-3, specifically focusing on the fruit of salvation: love (2:9-10). And with the horizontal relationship with each other in 4-5 as he gives the believer further evidence of his salvation.

I John 2:25
The Promise: Eternal Life

Here John identifies precisely what element of the New Covenant pertains to the church:

> **And this is the promise which He Himself made to us: eternal life. (2:25)**

This ensures the distinction of the church from Israel, but also gives the believer the assurance that God will keep His promise. And in light of John's stated purpose achieves the goal of bringing about true knowledge of assurance (5:13).

II John   80-85 AD

II John: Walking in Truth	1-3	The Knowledge
	4	The Faithfulness
	5-6	The Commandment
	7-11	The Opposition
	12-13	The Salvation

Background & Content

John refers to himself as the elder, and addresses his second letter to "the chosen lady and her children" (1:1), either referring to a woman or a church. Most probably the reference is to a church (12; III John 9). The probable date of this writing is between 80-85 AD.

John writes to commend the lady for her children walking in truth, by virtue of obedience to the commandment to love one another (5), and cautions against wandering from Christ's simple teachings (9).

III John   80-85 AD

III John: Walking in Truth - Hospitality	1-2	Salutation
	3-5	The Faithfulness
	6-8	The Allies: Brethren & Strangers
	9-11	The Opposition: Diotrophes
	12	The Ally: Demetrius
	13-14	Salutation

Background & Content

John writes his third epistle to an individual named Gaius. That name appears several times during Paul's ministry (Acts 19:29; 20:4; I Cor. 1:14), but it seems unlikely that the recipient of John's letter would be identifiable with them. It does seem that Gaius was a member of the church to whom II John was addressed (9), and the date of writing came after that of II John, sometime between 80-85 AD.

John writes to commend Gaius for walking in the truth, specifically by showing hospitality to brethren – even those who are strangers (6-8). He also reprimands Diotrephes for walking in contrast to the truth (9-11).

It is evident through John's epistles that the proof of the knowledge of the truth is a walk in the truth which is a walk of love and hospitality.

CHAPTER XI

PROMISES FULFILLED
THE SUMMATION

```
┌─────────────────────────────────────────────────┐
│                                                   │
│                    ? - Eternity                   │
│                                                   │
│                                                   │
│           The Revelation of Jesus Christ          │
│                                                   │
│      ┌──────────────────────────────────────┐     │
│      │                                      │     │
│      │          John's Apocalypse:          │     │
│      │        The Book of Revelation        │     │
│      │                                      │     │
│      └──────────────────────────────────────┘     │
│                                                   │
└─────────────────────────────────────────────────┘
```

Key Fulfillments

The Conclusion Of The Church -----------------Revelation 1-3
The Tribulation -------------------------------------Revelation 4-18
The Return Of Christ With His Church --------Revelation 19
The Kingdom Initiated ------------------------Revelation 20:1-6
The Ushering In Of Eternity ------------Revelation 20:1-22:21

Revelation   85-95 AD

Revelation 1-11: The New Covenant Fulfilled					
	1	The Things You Have Seen: The Commission of John			
	The Things Which Are 2-3	Letters to the Seven Churches	2:1-7	To Ephesus	
			2:8-11	To Smyrna	
			2:12-17	To Pergamum	
			2:18-29	To Thyatira	
			3:1-6	To Sardis	
			3:7-13	To Philadelphia	
			3:14-22	To Laeodicea	
	The Things Which Shall Take Place After These Things (part 1) 4-11	The Book and the Lamb: The Seven Seals	4 The Twenty Four Elders & the Four Beasts		
			5 The Lamb Worthy To Open The Book		
			6:1-2	1st Seal: Conquering	
			6:3-4	2nd Seal: War	
			6:5-6	3rd Seal: Famine	
			6:7-8	4th Seal: Death	
			6:9-11	5th Seal: Martyrs Cry For Vengeance	
			6th Seal 6:12-7:17	6:12-17 Earthquake/Catastrophe	
				7 The Remnant (Israel/Nations)	
			7th Seal (7 Trumpets)	8:1-7	1st Trumpet: Scorched Earth
				8:8-9	2nd Trumpet: Scorched Sea
				8:10-11 3rd Trumpet: Wormwood	
				8:12-13 4th Trumpet: Darkness	
				9:1-12 5th Trumpet: The Abyss	
				9:13-11:14 6th Trumpet: Army/Book/Witnesses	
				11:15-19 7th Trumpet: Kingdom Approaches	

Revelation 12-22: The New Covenant Fulfilled

The Things Which Shall Take Place After These Things (part 2) The Panorama

Pre-Tribulation 12:1-5		12:1-2	The Woman (Israel)
		12:3-4	The Dragon (Satan)
		12:5	The Male Child (Christ)
Early Tribulation 12:6-16		12:6	The Woman Protected
		12:7-16	Michael Wars With the Dragon
Latter Tribulation 12:17-14:20		12:17	The Dragon Enraged
		13:1-10	The Beast From the Sea
		13:11-18	The Beast From the Earth
		14:1-5	The Lamb and the 144,000
	The 3 Angels	14:6-7	Proclaiming the Gospel
		14:8	Destruction of Babylon
		14:9-12	Destruction to Beast Worshippers
		14:13	Blessing
		14:14-20	Reaping
Conclusion Of the Tribulation 15-19	The 7 Angels / The 7 Bowls of Wrath	15	Their Commission
		16:1-2	1: Malignant Sores
		16:3	2: Polluted Sea
		16:4-7	3: Polluted Waters
		16:8-9	4: Scorching Sun
		16:10-11	5: Darkness & Pain
		16:12-16	6: Assembling at Armageddon
		16:17-19:4	7: Judgment of Babylon
		19:5-10	Marriage of the Lamb
		19:11-16	The 2nd Coming
		19:17-21	Armageddon
20:1-6			The Millennial Kingdom
20:7-10			Satan's Last Stand
20:11-15			Final Judgment: The Great White Throne
Eternity 21-22		21:1-8	New Heaven & New Earth
		21:9-22:5	New Jerusalem
		22:6-21	Conclusion

Key Fulfillments

The Conclusion of the Church ------------------Revelation 1-3
The Tribulation --------------------------------Revelation 4-18
The Return of Christ With His Church --------Revelation 19
The Kingdom Initiated -----------------------Revelation 20:1-6
The Ushering in of Eternity ------------Revelation 20:1-22:21

Background

The apostle John was the last surviving apostle[75], and while he had been spared martyrdom, he still suffered an exile at the island of Patmos (1:9) at the hands of the emperor Domitian. It was during this exile that he wrote the Revelation, between 85-95 AD, making it the last component of Scripture. It is evident that John was set apart for the special task of recording this Revelation (John 21:20-24).

Notably, this is the only book that offers a blessing to those who read, hear, and heed the words of the prophecy (1:3; 22:7), as well as a curse for adding to or taking away from the words (22:18-19)

Many have failed to grasp the meaning of the book by attaching an allegorical meaning to the text, but a literal interpretation will unveil a clear message of the final fulfillments of the Promises of God.

Summary

The outline for the book is found in the commission of John, given in 1:19:

> Write therefore the things which you have seen, and the things which are, and the things which shall take place after these things.

Revelation 1
The Things Which You Have Seen

John records a stunning vision of the Messiah King who commissions him to write.

Revelation 2-3
The Things Which Are

Revelation 1-3
The Conclusion of the Church

These letters are written to actual churches in Asia Minor. To Ephesus: Christ commends their perseverance, yet rebukes them for leaving their first love (2:1-7). To Smyrna: He encourages them to overcome during times of tribulation (2:8-11). To Pergamum: He commends their faithfulness to Him, but rebukes their tolerance of false teaching and calls them to repentance (2:12-17). To Thyatira: as to Pergamum, He commends their faithfulness, while rebuking their tolerance for false teaching (specifically the prophetess, Jezebel), and encouraging them to persevere (2:18-29). To Sardis: He partially commends their deeds, but rebuking them for lacking spiritual life, challenging them to repentance (3:1-6). To Philadelphia: He has no rebuke, but only commendation and a call to perseverance (3:7-13). And finally, to Laodicea: He warns them of the judgment for being lukewarm. This is a 'church' of unbelievers, that has not yet received the riches of eternal life (3:14-22). This is commonly referred to as the apostate church.

While these are most certainly literal church bodies, some have speculated plausibly that the churches also represent various ages of church history. This seems likely, as the characteristics of these churches and the epochs of church history agree remarkably.

These letters comprise the last mention of the church until she appears in heaven and returns with Christ, pure and refined (Rev. 19:11-16). It is clear that the rapture removes the church from earth before the following period of tribulation (John 14:3; I Thess. 4:13-18; I Cor. 15:50-58) that is designated as Jacob's Trouble (Jer. 30:7).

Revelation 4-22
The Things Which Shall Take Place After
These Things

Revelation 4-18
The Tribulation: Jacob's Trouble

John records the events that will take place during Jacob's Trouble (Jer. 30:7), and Daniel's 70th week (Dan. 9:24-27), the latter half of which Christ called the great tribulation (Matt. 24:15-31). The events have the twofold purpose of refining Israel for her coming King, and judging the world for its wickedness.

The judgments include the seven seals, seven trumpets, seven angels, and the seven bowls of wrath. Daniel's fourth kingdom (the Roman Confederacy) is judged for evils comparable to those of Babylon (17-18).

Even in times of the most severe judgment, God protects Israel (12) and gives opportunity to repent (14:1-5).

Revelation 19
The Return of Christ with His Church

Christ returns, with the church, triumphantly (19:11-19). He judges the antichrist and his false prophet with those who had received antichrist's mark and worship him (19:20-21).

Revelation 20:1-6
The Kingdom Initiated

In keeping the Davidic Promises (II Sam. 7), Christ returns to the earth, and after imprisoning Satan (20:1-3), He takes His place on the throne of David, presiding for one thousand years in the Kingdom that Ezekiel described (Ezekiel 37-48), as the Messiah King prepares for the ushering of eternity.

Revelation 20:7-22:21
The Ushering in of Eternity

After the release of Satan and his final failed rebellion and judgment (20:7-10), Christ, at His Great White Throne Judgment, judges all whose names were not written in the book of life, according to their deeds (20:12, 15). Those deeds, of course, would be unsatisfactory to God, as faith is required to please Him (John 3:16; Heb. 11:6), and therefore, those judged would be cast into the lake of fire (20:15).

God does away with heaven and earth, replacing them with a new heaven and earth (20:11; 21:1) never to be stained by sin. Meanwhile, the city of New Jerusalem comes down out of heaven (21:2-21), becoming the center of worship for the Messiah King (21:2-22:5). These things marked the fulfilling of all of God's promises to Abraham (Gen. 12:1-3), of a great nation and worldwide blessing; to David. (II Sam. 7), of an eternal Kingdom; and also the fulfilling of the New Covenant (Jer. 31), which promised an eternal restoration of Israel, physically and spiritually, and promised the forgiveness of sins.

Jesus closes His Revelation given to John, with an assurance of His identity as the Fulfillment of the Covenants (22:12-13, 16), and a promise that He would indeed return (22:20). *God keeps His promises, to the praise of His glory.*

> *And let the one who is thirsty come; let the one who wishes take the water of life without cost.*   Revelation 22:17

Notes

[1] John Calvin, *Institutes of the Christian Religion* (Grand Rapids: Eerdmans, Mi. 1995), 64

[2] Ex. 17:14, 24:4, 34:27, Num. 33:1-2, Deut. 31:9

[3] Josh 1:8, 8:31, I Kings 2:3, II Kings 21:8, Ezra 6:18, Neh. 13:1, Dan. 9:11-13, Mal. 4:4

[4] Mt. 8:4, 19:7-8, Mk. 1:44, 7:10, 10:3-5, 12:26, Lk. 5:14, 16:29-31, 24:44, Jn. 5:45-46, 7:19-22

[5] Gleason Archer, *A Survey of Old Testament Introduction* (Chicago: Moody Press, 1994) 113

[6] Jamieson, Fausset, & Brown, *Bible Commentary, Job-Malachi,* (Peabody, Ma: Hendrickson, 2002), viii

[7] Gleason Archer, *The Encyclopedia of Bible Difficulties* (Grand Rapids, MI: Zondervan, 1982), 236

[8] Jamieson, Fausset, & Brown, *Bible Commentary, Job-Malachi,* (Peabody, MA: Hendrickson, 2002), 86

[9] Keil & Delitzsch, *Commentary on the Old Testament*, Jeremiah & Lamentations (Peabody, MA: Hendrichson, 2001), 232

[10] Robert Hubbard Jr, *First & Second Kings* (Chicago, IL: Moody Press, 1991), 11

[11] Samuel Schultz, *The Old Testament Speaks* (New York: Harper & Row, 1970), 286

[12] Keil & Delitzsch, *Commentary on the Old Testament*, Psalms (Peabody, MA: Hendrichson, 2001), 10

[13] Derek Kidner, *Psalms 1-72*. (London: Intervasity Press, 1973), 37-43, and Holman, *New American Standard Bible* Intro to Psalms, 456

[14] Gleason Archer, *A Survey of Old Testament Introduction* (Chicago, IL: Moody Press, 1994), 335

[15] John Walvoord, *Major Bible Prophecies* (Grand Rapids, MI: Zondervan, 1991), 271

[16] Dwight Pentecost, *Things to Come* (Grand Rapids, MI: Zondervan, 1958), 230

[17] *Ryrie Study Bible* notes, 1353

[18] Merrill Unger, *The New Ungers Bible Dictionary* (Chicago, IL: Moody Press,1988), 925

[19] Keil & Delitzsch, *Commentary on the Old Testament*, Isaiah (Peabody, MA: Hendrichson, 2001), 22

[20] Gleason Archer, *A Survey of Old Testament Introduction* (Chicago, IL: Moody Press, 1994), 391

[21] R.K. Harrison, *Jeremiah & Lamentations* (Downers Grove, IL: Intervarsity Press, 1973), 195

[22] Gleason Archer, *A Survey of Old Testament Introduction* (Chicago, IL: Moody Press, 1994), 413

23 Hal Lindsey, *The Late Great Planet Earth* (Grand Rapids, MI: Zondervan, 1970) 64-65 & Mal Couch, *Dictionary of Premillennial Theology* (Grand Rapids, MI: Kregel, 1996), 124-125

24 Keil & Delitzsch , *Commentary on the Old Testament, Ezekiel* (Peabody, MA: Hendrichson, 2001), 507

25 Ibid.

26 Jamieson, Fausset, & Brown, *Bible Commentary, Job-Malachi,* (Peabody, Ma: Hendrickson, 2002), 429

27 An alternate view recognizes the decree as referring to Ezra 7, which would, according to the sun calendar, complete the 483 years at 26 AD, or according to the lunar calendar, end at roughly 20 AD. Either possibility would be an accurate fulfillment of the stated prophecy and timeline.

28 H.B. Hackett, ed., *Smith's Dictionary of the Bible* (Boston, MA: Houghton Mifflin & Co., 1892), 2009 & Josephus, 11:6:1

29 Thomas Constable, *Notes on Esther.* Sonic Light 2004, 1

30 Gleason Archer, *A Survey of Old Testament Introduction* (Chicago, IL: Moody Press, 1994), 479

31 Arnold Fruchtenbaum, *Israelology* (Tustin, CA: Ariel Ministries Press, 1993), 3

32 Charles Ryrie, *Basic Theology* (Wheaton, IL: Victor Books, 1989), 397

33Lewis Sperry Chafer, *Systematic Theology, Vol. 4* (Grand Rapids, MI: Kregel, 1993), 27

34 Pentecost, 65

35 Ibid., 201-202

36 Ibid., 72-73

37 Ibid., 98-99

38 Ibid., 114-115

39 Ibid., 128

40 Josephus; Cecil Roth; & *The Columbia Encyclopedia*

41 Josephus, 12:5:4

42 Jamieson, Fausset, & Brown, *Bible Commentary, Matthew-Revelation,* (Peabody, MA: Hendrickson, 2002), xxvii

43 adapted from chart: Robert Stein, *The Synoptic Problem* (Grand Rapids, MI: Baker, 1987), 274

44 A.T. Robertson, *A Harmony of the Gospels* (New York, NY: Harper & Row, 1950). 261

45 W. Grinton Berry, *Foxe's Book of Martyrs* (Old Tappan, NJ: Power Books), 9

46 AT Robertson, *Word Pictures In the New Testament Matthew & Mark* (Nashville, TN: Broadman, 1931), 249

47 G.A. Williamson, ed., Eusebius, *The History of the Church* (New York, NY: Barnes & Noble Books, 1995),88

48 Ibid., 152

[49] Ibid., 265

[50] *Foxe's Book of Martyrs*, 7

[51] Eusebius, 109

[52] AT Robertson, *Word Pictures In the New Testament: Luke* (Nashville, TN: Broadman, 1931), ix

[53] Unger, 788 & *Smith's Dictionary of the Bible*, 1693

[54] Unger, 968

[55] Homer Kent, *The Pastoral Epistles* (Salem, WI: Sheffield Publishing Co., 1993), 243

[56] Eusebius, 104 & *Foxe's Book of Martyrs*, 13

[57] Eusebius, 72

[58] Unger, 650

[59] Mal Couch, *A Bible Handbook to the Acts of the Apostles* (Grand Rapids, MI: Kregel, 1999), 345

[60] J.B. Lightfoot, *St. Paul's Epistles, St. Paul's Epistle to the Galatians* (Peabody, MA: Hendrickson, 1995), 9

[61] F.F.Bruce, "Galatian Problems. 4. The Date of the Epistle," *Bulletin of the John Rylands Library* 54 (Spring 1972): 251.

[62] Robert Picirilli, *Paul the Apostle* (Chicago, IL: Moody Press, 1986), 156

[63] Martin Luther, *Commentary on Romans* (Grand Rapids, MI: Kregel, 1976), Preface

[64] W. Hendriksen, *The Epistle to the Philippians* (Banner of Truth, 1963), 7

[65] Unger, 1002

[66] Merrill Tenney, *New Testament Survey* (Grand Rapids, MI: Eerdmans, 1985), 358-359

[67] F.F. Bruce, *The Canon of Scripture* (Downers Grove, IL: Intervarsity Press, 1988)

[68] Leslie Church, ed., *NIV Matthew Henry Bible Commentary in One Volume* (Grand Rapids, MI: Zondervan, 1992), 723

[69] AT Robertson, *Word Pictures In the New Testament: John & Hebrews* (Nashville, TN: Broadman, 1931), 329

[70] Norman Geisler & William Nix, *A General Introduction to the Bible* (Chicago, IL: Moody Press, 1986), 385-408

[71] Merrill Tenney, *New Testament Survey* (Grand Rapids, MI: Eerdmans, 1985), 345

[72] Eusebius, 104 & *Foxe's Book of Martyrs*, 13

[73] Recognized at the Third Council of Carthage, AD 397

[74] AT Robertson, *Word Pictures In the New Testament: General Epistles* (Nashville, TN: Broadman, 1931), 201

[75] Eusebius, 128

Special Thanks

To Ralph, Lucy, & K.C. Cone,
When I glance at the pages of Scripture, I am reminded of your gift to me. You taught me to love the Lord and to cherish His Word. There is no greater gift that parents and a brother could have given. My heart has been shaped by your examples and by your love. I only pray that I could be such a blessed influence to others. I owe to you a debt of love.

With love and affection,

Your son & your brother

Bibliography

1. John Calvin, *Institutes of the Christian Religion* (Grand Rapids, MI: Eerdmans, 1995)
2. Keil & Delitzsch , *Commentary on the Old Testament.* (Peabody, MA: Hendrichson, 2001)
3. Norman Geisler & William Nix, *A General Introduction to the Bible* (Chicago, IL: Moody Press, 1986)
4. Gleason Archer, *A Survey of Old Testament Introduction* (Chicago, IL: Moody Press, 1994)
5. AT Robertson, *Word Pictures In the New Testament 6 Vol.* (Nashville, TN: Broadman, 1931)
6. Paul Benware, *Survey of the Old Testament.* (Chicago, IL.: Moody Press, 1988
7. H.B. Hackett, ed., *Smith's Dictionary of the Bible* (Boston, MA: Houghton Mifflin & Co., 1892)
8. Tim Dowley, *The History of Christianity* (Oxford, England: Lion Publishing, 1990
9. Jamieson, Fausset, & Brown, *Bible Commentary: 3 Vol.* (Peabody, Ma: Hendrickson, 2002)
10. Francis Andersen, *Job: An Introduction and Commentary* (Downers Grove, IL: InterVarsity Press)
11. C.D. Yonge, *The Works of Philo* (Peabody, MA: Hendrickson, 1993
12. Merrill Unger, *The New Ungers Bible Dictionary* (Chicago, IL: Moody Press,1988)
13. Robert Hubbard Jr, *First & Second Kings* (Chicago, IL: Moody Press, 1991)
14. Gleason Archer, *The Encyclopedia of Bible Difficulties* (Grand Rapids, MI: Zondervan, 1982)
15. G.A. Williamson, ed., Eusebius, *The History of the Church* (New York, NY: Barnes & Noble Books, 1995)
16. Merrill Tenney, *New Testament Survey* (Grand Rapids, MI: Eerdmans, 1985)
17. F.F. Bruce, *The Canon of Scripture* (Downers Grove, IL: Intervarsity Press, 1988)
18. J.B. Lightfoot, *St. Paul's Epistles, 4 Vol.* (Peabody, MA: Hendrickson, 1995)
19. Martin Luther, *Commentary on Romans* (Grand Rapids, MI: Kregel, 1976)
20. Robert Picirilli, *Paul the Apostle* (Chicago, IL: Moody Press, 1986)
21. Dwight Pentecost, *Things to Come* (Grand Rapids, MI: Zondervan, 1958)

22. Arnold Fruchtenbaum, *Israelology* (Tustin, CA: Ariel Ministries Press, 1993)
23. Robert Stein, *The Synoptic Problem* (Grand Rapids, MI: Baker, 1987)
24. Henry Thiessen, *Lectures in Systematic Theology* (Grand Rapids, MI: Eerdmans, 1992)
25. Charles Ryrie, *Basic Theology* (Wheaton, IL: Victor Books, 1989)
26. Hoerth, Mattingly, Yamauchi, *Peoples of the Old Testament World* (Grand Rapids, MI: Baker, 1994)
27. Samuel Schultz, *The Old Testament Speaks* (New York: Harper & Row, 1970)
28. Derek Kidner, *Psalms 1-72.* (London: Intervasity Press, 1973)
29. Derek Kidner, *Proverbs* (London: Intervarsity Press, 1964)
30. Michael Eaton, *Ecclesiastes* (Leicester, Britain: Intervarsity Press, 1983)
31. Desmond Alexander, David Baker, Bruce Waltke, *Obadiah, Jonah, Micah* (Downers Grove, IL : Intervarsity Press, 1988)
32. David Hubbard, *Joel & Amos* (Downers Grove, IL: Intervarsity Press, 1989)
33. *The Columbia Encyclopedia,* 6th ed. (New York: Columbia University Press, 2001–04)
34. David Baker, *Nahum, Habakkuk, Zepheniah* (Downers Grove, IL: Intervarsity Press, 1988)
35. R.K. Harrison, *Jeremiah & Lamentations* (Downers Grove, IL: Intervarsity Press, 1973)
36. Hal Lindsey, *The Late Great Planet Earth* (Grand Rapids, MI: Zondervan, 1970)
37. Leslie Church, ed., *NIV Matthew Henry Bible Commentary in One Volume* (Grand Rapids, MI: Zondervan, 1992)
38. Mal Couch, *Dictionary of Premillennial Theology* (Grand Rapids, MI: Kregel, 1996)
39. Thomas Constable, *Notes on Esther.* Sonic Light 2004
40. William Whiston, *The Works of Josephus* (Peabody, MA: Hendrickson, 1987)
41. Cecil Roth, *A History of the Jews* (New York, NY: Schockeh Books, 1989)
42. Mal Couch, *A Bible Handbook to the Acts of the Apostles* (Grand Rapids, MI: Kregel, 1999)
43. A.T. Robertson, *A Harmony of the Gospels* (New York, NY: Harper & Row, 1950)
44. Homer Kent, *The Pastoral Epistles* (Salem, WI: Sheffield Publishing Co., 1993)
45. Lewis Sperry Chafer, *Systematic Theology, 8 Volumes* (Grand Rapids, MI: Kregel, 1993)

46. F.F.Bruce, "Galatian Problems. 4. The Date of the Epistle," *Bulletin of the John Rylands Library* 54 (Spring 1972): 251.
47. www.bible.ca (maps)
48. W. Hendriksen, *The Epistle to the Philippians* (Banner of Truth, 1963)
49. John Walvoord, *Major Bible Prophecies* (Grand Rapids, MI: Zondervan, 1991)
50. W. Grinton Berry, *Foxe's Book of Martyrs* (Old Tappan, NJ: Power Books)